radical perversions:
two dyke plays by
AUDREY BUTLER

BLACK FRIDAY?
CLAPOSIS

women's PRESS

CANADIAN CATALOGUING IN PUBLICATION DATA

Butler, Audrey, 1959-
 Radical Perversions: Two Dyke Plays

ISBN 0-88961-156-4

I. Title

PS8553.U75R3 1990   C812'.54   C90-094722-5
PR9199.3.B87R3 1990

Copyright © 1990 Audrey Butler

All rights reserved. No part of this book may be used or reproduced in any manner whatsoever without written permission except in the case of brief quotations embodied in critical articles and reviews. For information address Women's Press.

Cover photo: Ruthann Tucker
Black Friday? photos: Mary Theresa Lawlor
Claposis photos: Donna Marchand
Design: Sunday Harrison
Copy editor/proofreader: Kate Forster

Published by Women's Press,
517 College St., #233, Toronto, Ontario M6G 4A2

This book was produced by the collective effort of Women's Press.

Women's Press gratefully acknowledges financial support from The Canada Council and the Ontario Arts Council

Printed and bound in Canada. First edition, July 1990

1 2 3 4 5   1993   1992   1991   1990

The quotation from Audre Lorde is taken from "The Transformation of Silence into Language and Action" in *Sister Outsider*, The Crossing Press/Trumansburg, New York 14886, The Crossing Press Feminist Series, 1984, at page 42.

PRINTED ON ACID-FREE PAPER

To Ma

Foreword

The lot of the woman playwright in Canada is not an easy one. The lot of the lesbian playwright is even more difficult. Much would have to change before a major theatre company – commercial or otherwise – would produce a play with the word "lesbian" in it, let alone a lesbian play. Still, Canadian lesbian playwrights do exist. Audrey Butler is one. And, like the characters in her plays, adversity has not stopped her.

Audrey's first play was produced in Cape Breton, her family's home for three generations. She began to write plays while a student at the University College of Cape Breton (UCCB). An English professor, Liz Boardmore, encouraged her to write for the UCCB Festival of New Plays. Her first two plays won prizes for the best original script: *Shakedown* in 1982 and *Cradle Pin* in 1983. Then Audrey moved to Toronto.

Being asked to write a script for the 1985 Buddies in Bad Times 4-Play Festival in Toronto was Audrey's leap into openly lesbian writing. Her *Claposis* is a romp through the hectic relationships between three women. It was well attended during its workshop production and at the 4-Play Festival six months later. Lesbians were, it seemed, hungry for plays including us, about us, and by us. Audrey was eager to feed that hunger. Since 1985, Audrey has re-written *Cradle Pin*, developing the relationship between the two female wrestlers into a love affair. She also wrote (and re-wrote and re-wrote and re-wrote!) *Black Friday?* And she has started a new play, *Medusa Rising*.

Claposis, Cradle Pin, Black Friday?, and *Medusa Rising* all include characters struggling with love, struggling with change, struggling with living in this crazy and often hostile world. Her characters live in the world with courage, with hope and with knowledge of the power of sexuality. Their relationships are taken for granted: a starting point, not something to be psychoanalyzed or explained away. They are who they are: no apologies.

These plays could not have been written in Cape Breton. To be able to write these plays, Audrey needed an environment in which she could hear her own words, see her work on stage and talk to people about what she was thinking. She needed to say, and hear, the word "lesbian" in public.

Often at Lesbian and Gay Pride Day in Toronto, Audrey meets friends from Cape Breton – people like herself, who could not be who they were without leaving home. Most of the characters in Audrey's plays are people who have left home, people trying to build a new home, one where they can be who they are.

This book includes only two of Audrey Butler's plays. *Claposis*, the earlier play, involves only young lesbians and looks mainly at their relationships with one another. The characters in *Black Friday?* are of different ages and sexualities, come with histories, and live in a world that surrounds and affects them. The differences between the two plays reflect changes in Audrey. In early 1986, Audrey came out to her family. She has been out publicly in the media several times since then.

Sexual orientation has been prohibited as grounds for discrimination in Ontario since 1986. But legal protection and increasing visibility of lesbians does not guarantee our acceptance. Major theatre companies are still evasive about producing lesbian plays. What are they afraid of? Perhaps they only mirror the fear that is visible – and more sinister – in other places.

Police mutter "dyke" as they push women aside at a pro-choice rally against the government's abortion bill. A police officer charges a drag queen for not wearing a seat belt in the back seat of a taxi. Police charge several dykes with assault, and at the same time charge only one of the men who attacked them. Police entice and entrap gay men in washrooms. Police officers wait outside of women's bars and follow lesbians home, taunting "Is that your girlfriend?" All of these incidents touched people directly or indirectly involved with the recent production of *Black Friday?* All happened within months of that production.

Audrey's plays may not change the violence and intolerance with which many people and institutions react to homosexuality. What her writing does show is that our sexuality is part of our lives. If that is radical, if that is perverse, it is not us who make it so.

TANNIS ATKINSON
TORONTO, MAY 1990

BLACK FRIDAY?

Overleaf:
Marie Bridget Dundon as "Rita"
Kate Johnston as "Terry"

PHOTO BY MARY THERESA LAWLOR

PLAYWRIGHT'S NOTE

Before starting this note I dove into my beloved copy of Audre Lorde's *Sister Outsider* for the strength to just put pen to paper tonight. I went immediately to my favourite words: the words that inspired *Black Friday?*:
> "we fear the visibility without which we cannot
> truly live"

Black Friday?? is a coming-out story, a love story, a labour story, a labour of love. Coming out is an act of love, for ourselves and for each other. In coming out we name ourselves, and naming ourselves is an act of power. The power of love is what I strive to write about and live through in a time of war. The mainstream theatre beat refused to review *Black Friday??* and nobody was surprised. The forces of silence have never been so blatant.
> Fear of being silenced.
> Fear of being rendered invisible.
> Fear of being visible.

These were my demons; they kept me going and held me back while writing this play. I was on the brink of exhaustion when I started this last rewrite, again. Tired and hungry again. The people who did this play with me kept me going.

If Terry were me right now she'd feel like she just gave birth. My midwife/director/dramaturge/best bud Bryden pulled me though. His patience with my "process" was astounding. Basically, my "process" involves indulging in every so-called "vice" known to human-kind until I'm feeling out on a limb, emotionally, spiritually, physically, before any creative explosion is possible, before everything "clicks" into place. The same way Bryden works, actually.

Throughout this process, really a "tempermental journey" (we named our theatre company well), I took many a wrong turn, followed numerous false trails, looking for a way, a voice, to say what I wanted to say, but Bryden, Kate, Marcia, Marguerite, Grant, Marie and Merle kept me on track, made it possible to say what had to be said. Along the way I was inspired by the enthusiasm of the play's crew and the visions of the play's designers. They are as much a part of this play as I am, some of the best lines are their lines, and their visions crystallized my own. It is through them and their acts of love, care and generosity that *Black Friday??* was made possible.

It's been a hell of a journey so far. It always is when you're a spiritual warrior/radical faerie, sexually erratic playrite/bulldyke aligned against the military-industrial complex that is poisoning our planet, our earth, our mother. That feeds our fears. That threatens to silence us.

Like love, the power of theatre changes us; to imagine a world without theatre is to imagine a world without love. But theatre has to change, the world must change, we must change. Without change we die. In my years as a semi-self-produced playrite no mainstream theatre has dared to produce any of my plays. This is understandable and their loss. This publication is dedicated to those of you who took the chance, participated in my "process" over the years and through umpteen rewrites, to those of you with the love and energy to put this play where all plays ultimately live and do their work of changing hearts and minds: on the stage where it belongs.

> AUDREY BUTLER, PLAYWRIGHT
> CO-ARTISTIC DIRECTOR, TEMPERMENTAL JOURNEY
> 5:00 A.M., MAY 21, 1990
> TORONTO, ONTARIO, CANADA

DIRECTOR'S NOTE

Audrey Butler didn't come out of the closet—she blew it up.

I had been in Toronto a year and already experienced my first baptism of fire at the hands of the theatre community when Audrey arrived at my door from our home—Cape Breton Island. We decided a cocktail was in order.

Bryden: Where should we go?
Audrey: Oh—I don't know.
Bryden: Hmm. I think I know a place you'll like.

We hit Church Street and entered a bar which, at the time, was called "Together"—a dyke bar that I attended regularly when I needed alternate sexual energy but wasn't into cruising or being cruised. Audrey sucked in the room like a sponge, eyeing each woman as if she were a present under a mammoth xmas tree. She turned to me and whispered, almost afraid of her own voice, "Thank you." I ordered the first vodkas. Things haven't been the same since.

We all have our coming-out stories—on a variety of levels. But, unfortunately, in this society coming out sexually is not realized as the celebration it should be. Instead, it is far too painful and far too lonely—cruel, almost, as there is always someone watching who knows exactly what is happening, but for one reason or another refuses to acknowledge it for what it is: a private, frightening metamorphosis.

Once through this first set of wringers, we as writers know instinctively that we must write about it—we have to take it back home.

Claposis, though written first, is after the fact—a crisp, quirky love triangle that plays with sexuality like a kitten with a ball of yarn. But *Black Friday?* is where it all began, and Audrey knew she had to go back there at some point.

When we decide to come out on paper we are told immediately (usually by straight people or by gay people who have yet to confront the issue themselves) that these stories are impossible to translate to the page or the stage, but we who know differently dive into the middle of the madness until we are up to our tits in intimacies screaming for sanctuary. So we start to add things—fire eaters, flamenco dancers, video screens, collapsing walls, etc.—to enhance this painful simplicity. Then we start to come out all over again and begin to take things away, and every word we write is like the first word we've written. Such was the

Tempermental Journey Audrey and I embarked on quite some time ago.

Black Friday? is a lovely play, a nice play, a simple play that wants only to tell the truth. And Audrey has accomplished this telling beautifully while at the same time cleaning out some dusty cupboards to make room for more intimacies, more truths, more plays!

Working with Audrey on *Black Friday?* has been the quintessential labour of love, and I am right friggin' proud to have been around to witness this particular closet exploding.

> BRYDEN MACDONALD
> CO-ARTISTIC DIRECTOR, TEMPERMENTAL JOURNEY

PRODUCTION NOTES

The seeds of *Black Friday* (without title and question mark) were planted seven years ago before leaving Cape Breton and moving to Toronto. The seedlings came to the surface while participating in the Six Playwrights' Unit at Tarragon Theatre, Toronto, five years later. The first public reading at Tarragon's Maggie Bassett Studio in November of 1987 opened many doors of perception and raised more questions than it answered – questions that needed to be asked.

Over the course of the following year I took peeks at the script, rethinking it, rewriting bits now and then with Bryden MacDonald's encouragement and suggestions. Janine Fuller approached me about submitting it to Nightwood Theatre's Groundswell Festival, where it was workshopped with a fine hard-working cast and a first-time director, Karen Woolridge. This is where Marcia Johnson first took on the role of Spike.

Black Friday's (still without the question mark) inclusion in Buddies in Bad Times Theatre's fourth Annual 4-Play Festival of Lesbian and Gay Works in April of 1989 was the beginning of an intensive workshop process which eventually led to where the script is now, where I literally rewrote the last three pages hours before the first preview. The actors rehearsed and Bryden blocked it in front of CBC cameras, there to tape a snippet for their coverage of the Festival on the six o'clock news.

Black Friday, the workshop production, premiered the next night with the following cast:

TERRY	....	Kate Johnston
SPIKE	....	Marcia Johnson*
EFFIE	....	Marguerite MacNeil
RITA	....	Merle Matheson*
RODDY	....	Grant Carmichael*

Directed and designed by Bryden MacDonald

This version of the script was published in the February 1990 issue of *Theatrum: Canada's Theatre Magazine*.

The next step was a full production, so Bryden and I formed our company, Tempermental Journey. The casting remained the same, except for the role of Rita, played by Marie Bridget Dundon* replacing another wonderful actor, Merle Matheson.

Black Friday? – question mark – premiered at Actors' Lab Theatre, Toronto, May 10, 1990. It was directed by Bryden MacDonald, with Christine Plunkett as set and costume designer, Veronica Macdonald as lighting designer/production manager, and Tracey Izatt as stage manager. This production would not have been possible without the financial assistance of the Ontario Arts Council, the Lesbian and Gay Community Appeal of Toronto and Buddies in Bad Times Theatre's Seed Show program, and the hard work of many people.

One of the most exciting aspects of the "process" this time around was working with a designer for the first time. Christine Plunkett's evocative set was based on an old photograph, the kind held in place by those corner mounts you can't get anymore. These corners were the steps into the "living room." Setting the play in the round was a primary consideration in the overall design, both physically realizing the journey motif of the play and putting the audience in the "picture."

Many people have asked: why the question mark? The short answer: it is a recognition of the double entendre in the title. Through the process of writing the play I began to perceive one of the characters as Black. Why? For me there was a clear connection between homophobia, racism, and the system that destroyed Terry's father. The title transcends a real historical event (my intention when I started the play) and encompasses issues I have been struggling with as a white working-class dyke. The challenge of writing this play was to bring them all together into one coherent theatrical whole. So what is *Black Friday?* It is a wind of change, a downfall, an uprising, it is anything that moves us into action, into coming out and coming together.

Although Tempermental Journey's production of *Black Friday?* cast Spike as Black and Terry, Effie, Rita and Roddy as white, this is by no means carved in stone. I support and encourage non-traditional casting and give future productions permission to change, alter or delete lines where appropriate in this regard.

AUDREY BUTLER

*Appeared courtesy of the Canadian Actors' Equity Association.

♦♦♦
BLACK FRIDAY?

A one-act play in six scenes, performed without an intermission.

Set in and around a living room in Cape Breton.

Intro music: "Jack to the Sound of the Underground" by Hithouse into Howie MacDonald's "Cape Breton Fiddle," selections of which are used during the lighting cues between scenes.

CAST OF CHARACTERS

TERRY: A woman in her early thirties, a spiritual warrior, Rita and Frank's prodigal daughter, returning home after a six-year absence.

SPIKE: A woman in her early twenties, the twenty-first century's first dyke philosopher, Terry's lover.

EFFIE: A woman in her late sixties, Rita's "aunt," but really her mother. They live together.

RITA: A woman in her mid-fifties, Terry's mother.

RODDY: A man in his mid-thirties, a professor and neighbour of Rita and Effie's. Also Terry's ex-lover, the first person she came out to.

SCENE ONE

Effie on her knees with curlers in her hair, moving furniture around and going over the carpet furiously with a miracle brush.

EFFIE: Holy-mother-of-god
where does it all come from?
Filth just piles up around here
like big jesus mountains–
effin' vacuum cleaner on the blink–

Enter Spike and Terry, both in bike leathers.

EFFIE: Old as Methusela!
Need two to handle this job–
They better start takin' their shoes off
that's all I can say–

Effie sees Spike, screams. Sees Terry, screams.

TERRY: Aunt Effie!
It's me!
Terry!
Terry from Toronto!

EFFIE: Jesusmaryandjoseph – Theresa!
Scared me half to death
in that outfit!

TERRY: Sight for sore eyes, eh!

EFFIE: You little shit!

TERRY: C'mere, sexy.
Give your brat a big hug!
They hug.

EFFIE: Not such a little brat anymore–
Look at you! A grown woman.
The twins are gonna bawl their eyes out.
Course they're not so little anymore–
goin' on sixteen!
And gorgeous just like their cousin–
Who's that?
Simultaneously

TERRY: SPIKE:
Sophie–   Spike.

TERRY: My roommate.
She drove me up.

EFFIE: Youse look like a pair'a martians.

SPIKE: Spike the bike dyke.

EFFIE: What was that, dear?

TERRY: Where is everybody?
Thought you'd have a houseful–

EFFIE: Took off out the bungalow right after work
Mary Catherine Elizabeth and the twins.
In your Uncle Jerry's new car.

SPIKE: Mary Catherine Elizabeth?
Who are they?

TERRY: Not they, she.
We call her Libby.

EFFIE: My sister Sadie's daughter.
Separated from her husband.

TERRY: Isn't that dizzy broad divorced yet?

EFFIE: I don't believe that one's ever gonna get divorced
to tell you the truth.
I'm glad they're all outta my hair
for a few days–
Get my spring cleaning done.

TERRY: The twins are Libby's; they all live here–

EFFIE: Since the twins were ten–
Crazy as a bag of hammers around here!

TERRY: Spike's gonna stay here.

EFFIE: Like my new TV?
Combination radio.
Your Uncle Jerry bought it for me Christmas.

TERRY: Bought it! Probably stole it.
Spike can stay in the attic with me–

(To Spike) My room's in the attic–

EFFIE: Like livin' in a cuckoo bird treehouse–
The twins are up there now.
Couldn't swing a cat in their old room.
They tormented us something awful–

TERRY: The twins in my room? Since when?

EFFIE: Since Christmas.

TERRY: Great!
We'll just sleep in their beds–
They're sleepin' out the bungalow, right?
They won't mind.

SPIKE: Oh goody, twin beds–
We'll switch back and forth each night–

EFFIE: If you can dig them out–
Room's filthy.

| | She was the same way–
never picked up after herself– |
|---|---|
| SPIKE: | She still doesn't. |
| TERRY: | Oink, oink. |
| EFFIE: | Oh, go ahead–
The twins won't mind. |
| SPIKE: | Great! |
| EFFIE: | You're not upset, are you, Terry?
About your attic? |
| TERRY: | Naw – it's okay. |
| EFFIE: | Attics are for ghosts and mad wimmin–
I'm surprised Rita let the twins
move up there–

That attic room of yours was like a shrine to her–
But that girl is fulla surprises! |
| TERRY: | Where is Ma?
She teaching? |
| EFFIE: | She never even breathed a word you were comin'! |
| TERRY: | Nobody knows. |
| EFFIE: | Lose another job didja.

Spike laughs. |
TERRY:	No, I quit.
SPIKE:	Oh, Terry, they were gonna fire you anyway.
TERRY:	Because I told that jerk of a manager off–
EFFIE:	She takes right after her father, this one.
Bad as the day is long.
TERRY:	Did Ma go out to the bungalow?
EFFIE:	Never did a lick of work–
TERRY:	Is she out shopping?
EFFIE:	Left Rita high and dry–

TERRY: Visiting?

EFFIE: Never sent so much as a Christmas card.

TERRY: I sent you a card!
I even sent Libby a card–
And you know how much I love her.

EFFIE: I'm talkin' about your father – Frank.
I'd never thought I'd say this
but we need a man like Frank around here now.
Just look at those poor people in Canso
losin' their fish plant!
A whole town!
Wiped off the face-of-the-earth!

TERRY: Damn right, Aunt Effie–

EFFIE: As far as I'm concerned
they shoulda shut down that steel plant years ago–
givin' us hope in the one hand,
snatchin' it away with the other!
The years your father was blacklisted:
He was a real rebelrouser!
He got people thinkin'.
Those were his glory years
but that was way before Black Friday.
He shoulda left then while the goin' was good!
But no!
He stuck around–
and gave us all nothin' but grief!

TERRY: I heard Cyril Bishop set him up.

EFFIE: Bullshit!
That story's been goin' around for years!
Cyril was heartbroken–
Cyril never framed your father–
He kept this family outta the poor house!
When Frank couldn't even keep food on the table!
Frank's biggest downfall was himself, dear.
Nobody drove Frank out but Frank.
Black Friday was just an excuse to
run out on you and your mother.

SPIKE: I don't know, Terry–
He was pretty pounded that night.

EFFIE: Lord above!
You've seen your father!

TERRY: Aunt Effie, I'm writing a story about him!
For a magazine back in Toronto.
And if it's really good,
they'll let me write more.

EFFIE: That's beautiful, dear.
Does it pay?

TERRY: Well, not at first.
That's why I'm here:
to get some of his stuff–
the boxes with the newspaper clippings–

EFFIE: Oh is that all you came back for?
What about us?

TERRY: Oh, Effie–

EFFIE: He better not show his face around here!

TERRY: Why would he?
All of his friends turned their backs on him.

EFFIE: Oh, Terry,
what's that man been filling your head with?
He doesn't have any friends left!

TERRY: Effie!
Where's Ma?
Don't tell me she left you here all on your own
for the weekend?

EFFIE: I wish she would!
I'm not your mother's keeper–

TERRY: Oh, for god's sake.
You and Ma on the outs again?

EFFIE: Spikey dear, you from the Pier?

TERRY: Effie!

SPIKE: Pier? What Pier?

TERRY: Sophie's from Toronto, Aunt Effie.

EFFIE: Whadda sin.
Been ages since your mother put my hair up–
Give me a hand, will you, dear–

TERRY: Sure–

> *Terry helps Effie take her curlers out.*

EFFIE: Your mother's been in a terrible state
since Christmas.
You turnin' down that plane ticket,
that's what started it all–
Ouch!

TERRY: I told her I had to work.
Hold still–

EFFIE: Same excuse the last three Christmases–

TERRY: I couldn't afford it all the other times–

EFFIE: Ah, Terry–
we coulda found the money–
scraped the the dough together somehow.
Good way to treat your mother!
After all she's done for you.
Half out of her mind with worry–
the goin's on in this family–
first her father–
then Libby leaving that no-good husband of hers–
movin' in with the two girls!
Place always in an uproar about something–

Still–
It's good to see you, dear.

> *Terry kisses the top of Effie's head.*

Oh, my,
this puts me back.
Old days at the shop–
had my own business, y'know.
The girls fussed around me like I was royalty
every time I got my hair done–
treated me just like a queen.
I was good to my girls, though,
and they were good to me.
Grab me that can down by your foot, dear.

TERRY: Diet coke?
Since when?

Rita enters, circles stage loaded down with groceries and a vacuum cleaner.

EFFIE: Went off regular for Lent.
Don't taste the same anyway.

RITA: *(Over Effie)*
Afternoon, Roberta–
paper towels on sale at Shopper's.
Yes, the damn thing is finally fixed–
charged me eighty-six bucks–
Effie'll have a field day.
Caught a whiff of your
lilies-of-the-valley last night–
heavenly.

EFFIE:
New Year's your mother had Jerry
over here – hauled your old bed back
up from the basement where we'd
put it before moving the twins–
set it up in the twins' old room.
She's been there ever since. That
room was supposed to be our
sewing room.

TERRY: You mean you and Ma aren't sleeping together anymore?

Enter Rita.

RITA: Terry!

TERRY: Ma!

They hug.

RITA: You didn't lose another job, didja?

Spike laughs.

TERRY: Ma, I quit, okay?

RITA: Horseshit.

(To Spike) Hi, I'm–

EFFIE: High time you picked that up–
it's been in the shop for weeks!

RITA: I woulda picked it up sooner
if you'd told me about it sooner!

EFFIE: I been telling you for weeks–

RITA: You been meaning to tell me for weeks,
that's what you said this morning when I left the house–

EFFIE: Oh, go away with ya!
I said no such thing–

SPIKE: When Terry started talkin' about headin' east,
I thought she meant Provincetown, not Cape Breton.
Hi, I'm–

TERRY: SPIKE:
Sophie–   Spike.

                                            You're Terry's mother?
                                            You look young enough to be her
                                            sister.

RITA: Spike?
You're Terry's–

TERRY: SPIKE:
Spike drove me up here–   We live together–

                                            Boy, the fog you guys get
                                            in this part of the world–
                                            soon as we hit Nova Scotia,
                                            felt like I was riding on a cloud–
                                            headlight cuttin' through it
                                            like a knife–

TERRY: We've been on the road all night–
where've you been?

RITA: Visiting Sister Theresa up the hospital–
she took a bad fall last week.
Too much communion wine.
She's the picture of her father–
always was.

TERRY: Ah, Ma.

        Effie turns on the vacuum cleaner.

RITA: Sister Theresa asked after you again, Aunt Effie.
When you gonna go see her?
Effie!
That's a sin.
Her own flesh and blood!

RITA: *(Running over to the machine, turning it off)*
Turn that damn thing off!

RITA: *(To Spike)* Sorry, dear,
Didn't mean to twist your ear off.

TERRY: I saw Dad.

RITA: Oh, you found your father.
I don't wanna have nothing to do with the likes of him—
even if he does come back.

Rita leaves and circles stage, Terry follows.

TERRY: He's not coming back.
You were all against him when he left—

RITA: Oh, is that your father's latest story?
'Cause if it is, he's stuck with it—

TERRY: It's the truth.
He saw Black Friday coming
and the union wanted him outta the way—

RITA: You don't have to recite it for me
chapter and verse, Theresa!
There were days when I couldn't go through that door
without giving myself a good talking-to—
screw up my courage just to face the day.

TERRY: How do you think I felt?
Got up to go to school one morning
and there's "commie bastard"
spray painted all over the front of our house.

RITA: Is that why you're here, dear?
To bring all that up again?

EFFIE: *(To Spike)* You sure you're not from the Pier, dear?

TERRY: I'm working on a magazine article
about Cape Breton's labor history—

RITA: Oh, Terry, you're not gettin' yourself mixed up
in that mess, are you?
Look what it's done to this family.

TERRY: Look, Ma, it's really important to me—

RITA: As far as I'm concerned that subject
is dead and buried
and it can stay that way—

TERRY: Ma, all I want are Dad's Dorchester columns
the ones he wrote for the Highland Press
the ones that got him blacklisted
the ones that got him sent to Dorchester prison
for sedition.

RITA: Well, dear.
You'll have to talk to Roddy Bishop.

TERRY: Roddy Bishop? Why?

RITA: I gave them to the Archives, dear.
That's the best place for them–

TERRY: Dad left those behind for me.
That's what you said!

RITA: I figured you didn't have any use for them anymore.

TERRY: When did this happen?

RITA: Months ago.
Christmas.
If you'd been around maybe I would've kept them.

TERRY: Ah, Ma, thanks for the plane ticket,
I really appreciated your offer–
I just had so much work–

RITA: Why didn't you quit your job then?

TERRY: Ma, I just don't like Christmas–

RITA: You coulda made the extra effort,
we're family, for crissake!

TERRY: I'm sorry.
Ma, I wish you hadn't given the columns to Roddy Bishop.
His uncle never lifted a finger
to defend Dad after Black Friday–

RITA: Cyril Bishop saved your father's name
dragged him outta the tavern
kept him in good with the union.
Cyril Bishop got your father outta Dorchester Prison–

TERRY: Frank says Cyril set him up–

RITA: Was he sober?
That story's been makin' the rounds for years.

Rita enters the living room,.Terry follows.

Roddy's been awful good to us since you left–

EFFIE: He's askin' after ya all the time–

RITA: Asked after you the other day–

SPIKE: Who?

RITA: Sorry, dear,
teacher out at the university–

TERRY: A professor, Ma.

EFFIE: Terry here was Teacher's pet–

TERRY: Teacher's assistant, Aunt Effie.

SPIKE: Oh, your old boyfriend.

RITA: What's that, dear?

TERRY: She's just teasing.

SPIKE: Oh, am I, now? Teacher's pet, huh?

TERRY: Don't start–

RITA: Theresa!
Go talk to Roddy, he still lives across the way–
He'll show you the Dorchester columns, I'm sure.

EFFIE: His Aunt Shirley,
she's been living it up in that new condo
for the last coupla years–
Oh, jezus, goin' concern, that one.
He owns that house now.
Shirley gave it to him!

Taps Terry's knee.

Still single!

Effie exits.

TERRY: I'll go see Roddy on my own time, okay?

RITA: You're as stubborn as Frank,

| | that's for sure.
Suit yourself, always have. |
|---|---|
| RITA: | *(To Spike)* Welcome to Cape Breton, dear. |
| | *Rita exits* |
| | *Terry takes out a flask, starts drinking.* |
| TERRY: | Welcome to the Twilight Zone. |
| SPIKE: | This is great! |
| TERRY: | You're kidding. Look at this place–
Graceland North. |
| SPIKE: | *(Picking up one of many snowbubbles)* I love these things. |
| TERRY: | You would.
Some of this stuff has been here since
my great-grandfather built it a million years ago– |
| SPIKE: | *(Picking up one of many photographs)*
This why you don't have pictures on the wall? |
| TERRY: | Cute, Soph ... that's him, the paranoid patriarch.
His daughters Sadie, Theresa and Effie.
Effie's not really my aunt.
Did I tell you that? |
| SPIKE: | So who is she? |
| TERRY: | She's really my grandmother–
My mother's mother– |
| SPIKE: | I thought Sadie was your grandmother. |
| TERRY: | She's really my aunt–
Effie had Mom out of wedlock. |
SPIKE:	But she's really your grandmother–
TERRY:	Who?
SPIKE:	Who are we talking about?
TERRY:	Sadie's called my grandmother–
SPIKE:	But she's really–
TERRY:	My aunt–
who was married to my Uncle Jerry–

SPIKE: The guy with the car.

TERRY: And then there's Libby's twins–

SPIKE: Who's Libby?

TERRY: Sadie's adopted daughter–
who was married to a real jerk–
The son of Uncle Jerry's best friend–
But nobody knew till afterwards–

SPIKE: What?
That he was the son of Uncle Jerry's best friend?

TERRY: No, that he was a jerk–

SPIKE: So who's Sister Theresa?

TERRY: A nun.

SPIKE: Jesus Christ!
But who is she?

TERRY: My aunt. A nun. And my aunt.
Her and Aunt Effie ran a hairdressing shop downtown–
"Chez Marie."

SPIKE: Who's Marie?

TERRY: Marie – Mary–

SPIKE: So who's Mary?

TERRY: The Virgin Mary–
They named the shop after her–

SPIKE: Who did?

TERRY: Effie and Sister Theresa–

SPIKE: I thought she was a nun, not a hairdresser.

TERRY: She is!
Didn't become a Bride of Christ until her forties–
Look at her in this picture – pretty hot, huh?
I think she's a dyke.
Anyway–
Effie ran the shop on her own for another twenty years
and Sadie brought up everybody's kids.

> Jesus, all these family secrets,
> Effie'd keel over if she knew I knew–

SPIKE: Knew what?

TERRY: That she's really my grandmother.

SPIKE: Honey–
How do you remember all this?

TERRY: Oh, and it gets even worse–
Night before Ma married Frank she got an anonymous note telling her Effie was really her mother–
He swears Effie sent it.

SPIKE: Why would she do that?

TERRY: Effie never wanted them to get married.
Frank wasn't Catholic–
Oh, god!
Thank god my mother rebelled–
I was almost Roddy's cousin–

SPIKE: What?

TERRY: If Effie had managed to set Rita up
with Cyril Bishop–

SPIKE: Never mind! Forget I even asked.

TERRY: Religion's fucked in the head anyway–
I stopped going to mass when I was sixteen–
Sister Theresa was convinced I'd end up the town slut–

SPIKE: She wasn't too far off the mark.
Whadda ya call these things?

TERRY: Snowbubbles.
I should just stay out of it–
Get those boxes I came for and leave.

SPIKE: As if you could.
Gimme a break.
And stop calling me Sophie.
I hate that name.

TERRY: I like it, it's cute.

SPIKE: Cute!

TERRY: You're a real softy, Sophie.

SPIKE: Am not.

TERRY: Are too.
I'll prove it.

SPIKE: Here? Now?

TERRY: Yup.

SPIKE: You wanna bet?

TERRY: Whaddya wanna bet, Sophie?

SPIKE: A tank of gas for the bike.

TERRY: How about a hot lube job.
Sophie.

SPIKE: A tank of gas for the bike.

TERRY: Lube. Head to toe.

SPIKE: Gas.

TERRY: Magic fingers massage.

SPIKE: You're on.

They start to wrestle. Terry drops Spike to the floor, they wrestle around on the carpet like a couple of kids. Spike turns it around.

TERRY: Dirty wrestler! Dirty wrestler!

Effie enters, picks up her curlers and diet coke.

EFFIE: *(Exits singing)* "Are you lonesome tonight..."

Terry jumps up.

TERRY: Shit!
I knew that would happen.

SPIKE: Relax, Terry–
she's cool.

TERRY: It's not that simple–

SPIKE: Oh, you wanna pretend we're just friends now.

TERRY: Just tone it down a little–

SPIKE: Tone it down a little?
How could you ask me that?

Effie and Rita entering the stage.

RITA: Aunt Effie!
Don't leave the room while I'm talkin'–

SPIKE: Why am I here? Shock value?

EFFIE: As far as I'm concerned,
Theresa stopped being my sister twenty years ago.
I wouldn't trust her as far as I could throw her.

RITA: I think it's about high time
you stopped this foolishness–

EFFIE: My own sister swindles me outta half my share
of the shop – has a vision in the middle of a blue rinse
and runs off with the nuns–

TERRY: Oh, Aunt Effie, not that again–

SPIKE: Are you sure this broad's a nun?
She sounds like "Kitten with a Whip."

TERRY: Aunt Effie, Sister Theresa put your share in trust–

EFFIE: You!
You're a good one to talk.
Couldn't pick up the telephone, tell us you were coming.
Coulda took something decent outta the freezer!

TERRY: It's okay, Aunt Effie. Don't go to any trouble.

EFFIE: All I got is last week's chicken stew.
Beef's so dear these days.
It's scandalous.
Cut off my right arm before I pay that price for it–

RITA: Then why don't you!

TERRY: Let's just all go out for Chinese.

EFFIE: You know how Chinese hates me!
Want me up half the night?

RITA: God forbid.

EFFIE: Oh, you're just here to stir up trouble!
She takes right after her father, that one.

RITA: Effie!
You've got no right shootin' your mouth off like that
in front of Terry – the girl hasn't been home twenty minutes!

Enter Roddy, circling stage pulling a vacuum cleaner with a stack of Elvis albums and an old photo album.

TERRY:	RODDY: *(Over the others)*
It's okay, Ma.	Hey, Donny.
	Is that the car you were telling me
RITA:	about? It's a heap of junk.
Shootin' her mouth off like that	Looks like a big waste of time to me.
in front of company–	Won't pass the inspection
	That pile of junk's giving you a
SPIKE:	hard time, not me.
Don't mind me!	Crazy bastard.

EFFIE: Say anything I want to in my own home!
Papa left this house to me, remember!

RITA: Here we go again–

TERRY: Will you two give it a rest!
I didn't come 1500 miles to listen to you two
fightin' like cats and dogs!

Enter Roddy on stage.

RODDY: Oh, well, look,
your vacuum cleaner's back–
Terry!

TERRY: Hi, Roddy.

RITA: I shoulda left ours in the shop–

RODDY: Effie called me,
wanted to borrow my vacuum cleaner.

EFFIE: Take your shoes off!

RODDY: They're clean.

Effie throws up her hands.

RITA: Might as well come in,
join the party–

EFFIE: Roddy darlin', that's beautiful,
you bringing that all the way over here.
God bless you.

RODDY: Welcome home, Ter.

TERRY: Hi, Roddy!

RODDY: I saw the big bike out back.
I thought it must be Terry!

RITA: Big bike?
Out back?

RODDY: *(To Effie)* Legion.
Tomorrow night.
How about it, sexy?

EFFIE: Ah, go away with ya!

RITA: Terry–

TERRY: Yeah, Ma.

RODDY: I hear they got three Elvises lined up.

32 / AUDREY BUTLER

RITA: Whose bike is out back?

EFFIE: You big tease!

SPIKE: *(Breaking through)* My bike!!!
Sorry.

RITA: Don't tell me you two came all the way up here on a motorbike!

TERRY: What did you expect, Ma?
The trains don't run to this end of the country anymore.
(Turns to Roddy) Roddy, this is my roommate, Spike. Spike, Roddy.

SPIKE: Hi.

RODDY: Hi.
How was the trip on a hog that size?

TERRY: Oh, god, you wouldn't believe–

SPIKE: *(interrupting)* Smooth ... and rough–
the fog was amazing, though.
There was one redneck town–
I thought we'd never get out alive–
wind up like those poor fuckers in *Easy Rider*–

TERRY: Ma, is the tea ready yet?

RITA: Come on, Effie–
Let's get that stew in the microwave–

Rita exits.

EFFIE: Just don't get me going or I'll stick you in the microwave–
Baked a pan of date squares yesterday, Roddy–

RODDY: Wouldn't miss them for the world, sweetheart.
Oh, look what I brought you.

Shows Effie the Elvis albums.

EFFIE: Oh, Roddy.
The King.

RODDY: Yeah, I found them in the basement.
And there's old photographs

of my great-grandfather and your father
in these albums.

EFFIE: *(Gives him a peck on the cheek)* Bless your heart, dear–

RITA: *(Offstage)* Effie!!

EFFIE: Lodge them over in my corner, dear–
we'll take a boo at them later.

   Effie exits.

RODDY: So, Terry–

TERRY: Roddy–

   They hug.

RODDY: This is what they're wearing in T.O. these days?

TERRY: They're bike leathers, Roddy.
We came all the way here just to make a fashion statement.

RODDY: Well, you'll get lots of attention around here.
If you two walk down Charlotte Street
you'll cause a ten-car pile-up!

Where did you two meet?
Don't tell me–
Canadian Tire!

SPIKE: The hardware department.

RODDY: I like her, Ter.
So, Spike.
"What's your father's name?"

SPIKE: What is he on?

TERRY: He's just happy to see me, darling.
Could you go get my knapsack–

SPIKE: I'll get it later–

TERRY: Now.
Please.

   Spike throws Terry a kiss as she exits.

RODDY: Your "roommate's" cute.

TERRY: Don't tell her that.

RODDY: She looks awfully young – is she jailbait?

TERRY: That's more your style, isn't it?

RODDY: Not since you broke my heart.
So what have you been up to?
Still writing, I hope.

TERRY: Actually, I'm working on a magazine article–
about labour unions on the Island.

RODDY: That's great!
Aren't you kinda out of touch with that in Toronto?

TERRY: Oh, it's been on my mind–

I saw Frank.

RODDY: Ohhh–
How's he doing?

TERRY: Great!
We talk to each other all the time.

Ma said she gave Dad's Dorchester columns
to the Archives–

RODDY: Yeah, isn't that great.
I put them all on microfiche last month.

TERRY: I'll need them to write.

RODDY: Yeah, sure.

TERRY: You still have the actual newspaper clippings?

RODDY: Yup.
Still in the boxes.

TERRY: Was there anything else in them?

RODDY: Like what?

TERRY: Letters?
Cards? For me?

RODDY: I don't think so.
But you're welcome to look.

TERRY: Frank said he wrote.
Said he's been trying to get in touch with me.

I thought there might be something mixed up in those boxes–
a birthday card or a letter.

RODDY: Was he sober?

Silence

Well, we should invite a few people over
for your homecoming–

TERRY: I'm just here to work.
And show Spike around.

RODDY: Remember when you dragged me into that
gay bar when we went to New York?

TERRY: Reading week.
A drag queen pinched your ass.
You'd think you never had your ass pinched before–

RODDY: Not by a man in a dress–

I was kinda disappointed–
you had lots of offers–
nobody gave me a second look–

TERRY: Everyone knew you were straight–

RODDY: I thought they liked that!
I thought I looked kinda sexy–

Terry laughs.

RODDY: Have you told Rita yet?

TERRY: No, not officially.
Ma wouldn't say "lesbian" if her mouth was full of one.

RODDY: You told me the night before we left for New York–
right after we made love.

TERRY: No!
Did I?

RODDY: You don't remember?

TERRY: Well, it was a long time ago.
It comes back every now and again–

RODDY: Yeah, like a bad penny.

Listen, Terry, I know I said a lot of awful things
the night before you left town–

TERRY: The fight about the dishes–

RODDY: The fight about the toothpaste–

TERRY: The fight about the union–

RODDY: The fight about the steel plant–

TERRY: The fight about the Cyril–

RODDY: The fight about the Frank–

TERRY: Frank says that Cyril set him up.
Did you know that?

RODDY: I've heard the stories–
Frank was in so much shit
he had to leave town.
Just ask Effie.

TERRY: Roddy–

RODDY: Terry, honey,
We all have to live with what Frank did–

TERRY: Cyril could have been lying. How do we know?
Maybe Frank was just the fall guy for Black Friday.

RODDY: Terry–

Spike enters, drops Terry's knapsack on the floor.

Sound of a teapot falling.

SPIKE: What the fuck was that?

TERRY: Ma!

RITA: Effie!

BLACKOUT/MUSIC

SCENE TWO

Later that night, Terry and Spike in a moonlit living room.. Terry is drinking.

SPIKE: Well.

TERRY: She's fine.
Fainted is all.
They're keepin' her in overnight.
Gonna run some tests in the morning.

SPIKE: What about Rita?

TERRY: She took it worse than Aunt Ef.
I just put her to bed.
God, those two are a pair.

SPIKE: Terry, you don't know how lucky you are.
Effie's a sweetheart.
And your mother is so–

TERRY: Unhappy.

SPIKE: Unhappy?

TERRY: All the time I was growing up I'd hear her down here crying
every time she had to leave the house–
she went through shit after Frank left.
People were really cruel.
I didn't know whether I was coming or going.
Twelve years old.
Effie's right–
I was a brat–

"Take right after your father!"
It's frightening.

Drinks from her flask.

I don't wanna upset Ma
but I have to write this article–
I think I'm just starting to realize
how far ahead of his time Frank was.
People just didn't understand–
They probably never will.

SPIKE: So you got some work done.

TERRY: I came across a coupla things in the attic–
pictures mostly.
Roddy's bringing over a coupla boxes tomorrow.
Even if I found one birthday card it would all make sense.

SPIKE: What would make sense?

TERRY: Something!
(Softer) Sweetie.

SPIKE: What if you don't find what you think
you're looking for?

TERRY: I won't think about that right now.

Silence

SPIKE: Terry – what is Black Friday?
What the fuck happened?

TERRY: Friday, October the thirteenth, 1967.
The day Frank's prediction came true.
All summer the steelworker's union
had been on the brink of splitting.
The membership was being asked to accept huge wage cuts.
People were being told they'd keep their jobs longer.
Frank was against it–
Cyril was for the cut.
Frank predicted disaster if it went through.
The vote came: Cyril won.
Two weeks later the steel plant shut down.
Once management split the union
they could do what they damn well pleased.
Black Friday.

SPIKE: It pisses me off.
The way people abuse the word black–
Black Friday black monday black market black clouds
over our heads
blacklisted
black black black...

TERRY: I know, sweetie–
you're right–

And me, right now I'm up to my ass in unions
and a father I barely knew.

Tomorrow I'm gonna go through
the Dorchester columns–

SPIKE: The stuff he wrote in prison?

TERRY: No, they sent him to prison
for writing them in the first place.
He had a column in the Highland Press
back in the early sixties
where he regularly goaded the masses
into revolution–
The union blacklisted him.

Spike reacts.

The bosses had him charged with sedition.
Of course the masses loved him at first
but when the crunch came they got scared.
He was just too smart for his own good.
Didn't take any shit either.

SPIKE: I had no idea Cape Breton was such a hotbed.

Terry, why am I here with you?

This isn't gonna turn into a dyke version of
"Guess Who's Coming to Dinner?" is it?

TERRY: You're here cause I want you here.

Terry kisses Spike.

SPIKE: When we left Toronto I was under the impression
that I was bringing you here
so you could give them the good news.
Now I don't even know if you're gay.

TERRY: Oh, would you like a signed affadavit?

SPIKE: Yes.

TERRY: Spike. What's gotten into you?

SPIKE: What's gotten into *me*?
What's gotten into you?

I don't recognize you anymore.
I shoulda stayed home.

TERRY: What?

SPIKE: Home. Toronto.
Where we live.

TERRY: You said you loved it here.

SPIKE: I do!
But I don't wanna move here and open a gay bar!
Terry! What's going on?
Effie's in the hospital, your mother's a nervous wreck and you're makin' moo eyes at this nutty professor guy–

TERRY: You're jealous.

SPIKE: Damn right I'm jealous.
Get your shit together, girl–
don't treat me like this.

I don't know what you're so afraid of.
My mother kicked me out when I was sixteen
when she found out I was dating girls.
Rita loves you.
I think she even likes me–

TERRY: How could she resist
"you look young enough to be Terry's sister"
You keep your hands off my mother!

Caresses Spike.

Has anyone ever told you you have
the sexiest, gooeyest, wickest, baddest,
hottest lips this side of Montreal?

SPIKE: Not lately.

They start making out.

TERRY: Soph.

SPIKE: What?

TERRY: Ma's bedroom is right at the top of the stairs.

SPIKE: I don't care–

TERRY: Soph.

Spike jumps up.

SPIKE: Does this mean–

TERRY: Shhhh–

SPIKE: Does this mean we won't have sex the whole time we're here?

TERRY: No, it just means–

SPIKE: What, Terry, what?

RITA: *(Offstage)* Terry!
Terry jumps up.

TERRY: Yes, Ma!

RITA: If you girls are hungry–
Spike tries to take Terry's leather chaps off, Terry fends her off.

TERRY: It's okay, Ma!
We're just gonna–
We'll be up soon–

RITA: If you girls get hungry through the night–
turn the stove off good–
those damn knobs stick–

SPIKE: I'll take a look at them, Rita–

RITA: Theresa, show her where the tools are.
Spike gets one leg unfastened.

TERRY: Okay!
Good night, Ma!

RITA: Good night, dear.
Oh, dear–

TERRY: Yes, Ma–

RITA: I'm making your favourite for supper tomorrow–
scalloped potatoes and baked ham–

TERRY: I'll be here, Ma.

RITA: Good night, dear.
Spike gets the other leg unfastened.
Goodnight ... Spike.

SPIKE: Goodnight, Rita.

TERRY: Tomorrow I'll do some work–
then we can relax and enjoy ourselves.

SPIKE: We could do that right now.

TERRY: Okay, okay,
I haven't been giving you enough attention lately–

SPIKE: Not nearly as much as I'm used to.

Spike unsnaps the chaps with her teeth, pushes Terry down onto the couch. They start making out.

LIGHTS FADE

BLACKOUT/MUSIC

SCENE THREE

Late the next morning, Terry going through newspaper clippings. Rita folding the laundry.

RITA: People have been feeling sorry for me for years.
They say I was so much like her when I was young
Sharp-tongued, headstrong, always wanting my own way.
Two peas in a pod.

TERRY: Who sent the anonymous note?

RITA: Cyril Bishop's mother sent it.

TERRY: You're kidding!

RITA: She didn't have much use for me after
I threw Cyril over for Frank.

TERRY: Tramp!

RITA: Theresa!

TERRY: What's this?

RITA: What in the name of god is that doing in there?

TERRY: I guess it got mixed up–
How old were you when this was taken?

RITA:	Seventeen.
TERRY:	"Rita McMillan thrilled audiences last night with a stirring rendition of Puccini's 'Madame Butterfly'"–
RITA:	I won first prize–
TERRY:	In the Kiwanis Music Festival.
RITA:	My dream was to go to the finals in Ottawa. What foolishness. Sister Theresa was my chaperone–
TERRY:	What?
RITA:	Never saw hide nor hair of her till we left to come back to Cape Breton. I placed fifty-four out of sixty. Two years later I married your father. That's what you did back then–
TERRY:	But you worked, damn right you worked, some of your students are singing professionally right now because of you–
RITA:	If I'm such a good teacher why am I still folding your laundry?
TERRY:	Ma, how can you stand it– living in the same house all these years– pretending Effie's your aunt–
RITA:	I didn't have much choice, Terry and most of all neither did she. We can't imagine what it must have been like back then– to have a child out of wedlock. To bring all that up now–
TERRY:	Do you know who your father is?
RITA:	Terry–
TERRY:	Who?
RITA:	One of two– Jimmy Morrison, who ended up a hermit in the woods– or Anthony Yakimachuk,

who owned the supermarket in the Pier.
Your grandmother was a pretty wild woman in her day.

TERRY: What's your favourite memory of Dad?

RITA: Terry–

TERRY: It couldn't all have been bad–

RITA: No, dear, it wasn't all bad.

TERRY: What about the day he came back from Dorchester?
You must've been ecstatic.

RITA: I felt like I'd never been kissed.

TERRY: What?

RITA: I was nervous, dear.
It had been a long time.

TERRY: I read where people from all over the Island
met him at the train station–

RITA: Frank's glory years–

He kissed you before he kissed me.

TERRY: Huh?

RITA: *(Touches her belly)* Here, dear–
I was eight months pregnant.

TERRY: Why didn't you tell me that before?

RITA: Sometimes you forget these things, dear.
Sometimes you have to.
Your father was such a handsome devil–
a real firebrand.
He'd give you the shirt off his back.
When he was president of the local
the phone never stopped ringing off the wall–
Frank couldn't say no.
We'd get calls in the middle of the night
and he'd be off, helpin' some poor soul.
Your father never stopped–
had to take a drink just to sleep
then a couple to just get through the day.
Once he started hittin' the booze

it was game over.

If it wasn't for Aunt Effie
slipping me a few bucks for groceries
when your father drank his paycheque
I don't know where we'd be.
Cyril was the sensible one–
Frank wanted the impossible.

TERRY: So why didn't you marry Cyril?

RITA: Don't get smart with me, young lady.

Enter Effie.

TERRY:
If you thought Dad was so awful–

RITA:
I loved your father–

TERRY:
If you loved Dad so much
why didn't you–

EFFIE:
(Over Rita and Terry)
Heart in my throat
all the way home–
Runnin' the red lights
like there was no tomorrow–
Taxi drivers!

RITA: What are you doing here?

EFFIE: I live here!

RITA: They finish all those tests this early?

TERRY: Let me take your coat–

EFFIE: They're all crazy up there–
Not gonna strap any machine on me and poke around–
For the love of God, all I did was faint.

RITA: Do you want me to call the hospital?

EFFIE: Suit yourself.

Exit Rita.

Watch my hair, dear.
Nice girl came in this morning
and did it for me.

TERRY: A candystriper?

EFFIE: No, a Newfoundlander.
Crazier than a KOC fleamarket up there.

	Take 'em weeks before they notice I'm gone. What's all this, dear?
TERRY:	Dad's Dorchester columns.
EFFIE:	What's this I hear about a book?
TERRY:	A book about the union–
EFFIE:	What about the union?
TERRY:	Well, depends on what I find–
EFFIE:	You'll find nothing but trouble!

Enter Rita with her spring overcoat.

RITA:	Effie, have a lay down before your shows.
EFFIE:	A cuppa tea won't hurt.
TERRY:	I'll bring you up one.
EFFIE:	*(To Rita)* Ah, dear, I want you to make me one.
RITA:	I have to go to visit Sister Theresa at the hospital!
EFFIE:	Cover for me–
RITA:	Then I have to make Terry's supper–
TERRY:	I'll take her upstairs, Ma–
EFFIE:	I don't need anybody takin' me up those stairs I been climbing them all my life!

Terry and Effie begin to exit.

EFFIE:	Rush rush RUSH.
TERRY:	Come on, Aunt Effie.
EFFIE:	I want my tea.
TERRY:	I'll bring you your tea–
EFFIE:	Sure, just stick me up the stairs, forget all about me–
RITA:	I don't wanna hear that kinda talk– you just got outta the hospital!

Rita gets ready to leave, starts to hum tentatively while putting on her lipstick. It's a recognizable snippet from Puccini's Madame Butterfly.

Spike enters, Rita reacts.

SPIKE: That was sweet.
Good as Leontyne Price.

RITA: Leontyne Price!
Oh, aren't you the comedienne.

SPIKE: I've seen her live three times–
that voice!
Makes the back of my head tingle,
my heart pound,
do somersaults in my chest.
Once I coulda swore
my womb swelled up to twice its size.

RITA: Oh!

SPIKE: Off to visit Effie?

RITA: Sister Theresa.
Oh, you haven't heard the latest:
Effie up and walked out of the hospital this morning–
more guts than brains, that one.
What are you up to, dear?

SPIKE: Changing the oil on the bike.
We really booted it up here–
wanna lift?

RITA: No no no no no–

SPIKE: Got the beast back together in no time.

RITA: Thanks, dear–

SPIKE: No problem.

RITA: What do you do up Toronto?

SPIKE: I work in a boozecan, bartending.

RITA: A blind pig.

SPIKE: Blind pig?

RITA: That's what we called them, dear.

Silence.

RITA: Have you two been friends for a while?

SPIKE: We met at the blind pig about a year ago.
A friend of hers was performing.
We have performers in once in a while.
He sang opera–
in drag–

RITA: Drag?

SPIKE: In a dress.

RITA: Sounds like a hoot!

SPIKE: Anyway,
I got off work–
Club doesn't close till six–
I go out to get on my bike and go home–
guess who's sittin' on her!
It was pissin' rain
but the sun was definitely on the rise.
She said "take me to the ocean"–
the best I could do was Lake Ontario.
Now I can't wait to see the ocean
the way Terry talks about it–

RITA: You should get her to take you to Kennington Cove–
best place to see the ocean.
Frank used to take us out there all the time.

Tell me something, dear.

Is Terry okay?

Is she drinking a lot?

SPIKE: Yeah–

RITA: Were you there when she met up with her father?

SPIKE: Frank was all over her.

RITA: Drunk?

SPIKE: *(Nods her head)*
She thought he was just wonderful.
I shouldn't be saying this–

but he was a mess. I couldn't believe
it was the same guy she told me about–
he went on and on about his glory years
whatever they were
told her he sent her all these cards
and wrote her all these letters–

RITA: That's impossible–
no mail came from Frank after he left–

SPIKE: He lied to her.

RITA: He's a coward–
I was always the "bad guy."
Frank could do no wrong as far as Terry was concerned–

SPIKE: Well, it looks like that's happening again.

Well, hey.
Let's hit the road.

RITA: Oh no no no no–
It's only a ten-minute walk.

SPIKE: I'll get you there in two–
I won't drive too fast.

Spike passes Rita a helmet as they exit.

RITA: Well, this will certainly be a first.
Effie would get a kick out of this–

SPIKE: I'll take her for a ride tomorrow.
What's this Pier she's always going on about?

RITA: Whitney Pier.
It's an area of town–

SPIKE: Where a lot of Blacks live–

RITA: Try not to mind her too much, dear.

BLACKOUT

SCENE FOUR

Later, Effie watching TV. Spike enters.

EFFIE: Holy-mother-of-god.
That is one smart dog.
Only show that's not fulla sex and dope–
Oh, hello, dear–
Where are you coming from?

SPIKE: Whitney Pier.

EFFIE: Smartass!

SPIKE: I'm serious.
I took Rita to the hospital–
She gave me directions.

EFFIE: All the coloured people there
came up from the Underground Railroad–

SPIKE: Yeah.

EFFIE: See anyone you know?

SPIKE: Smartass.

EFFIE: What's this book Terry's writing?
Am I in it?

SPIKE: A book about Frank–

EFFIE: Frank?
No one wants to read a book about a troublemaker!

SPIKE: Effie, does Terry have her facts straight?

EFFIE: Talk to Roddy–
I'm not saying no more.

SPIKE: Hey, I heard you pulled a fast one this morning–
walking out of the hospital like that–
were you scared?

EFFIE: Naw!
Fit as a fiddle I am.
Didn't wanna run into that no-good sister of mine–

SPIKE: I used to fight with my sister non-stop–
you haven't spoken in twenty years?

That's a long time to be mad at someone—
my sister was always giving me a hard time about something.

Enter Roddy

RODDY: Knock knock–
Everybody decent?

(*To Spike*) Hi.

SPIKE: Hi.

EFFIE: Roddy!
Seen more of you in the last two days than I have
in the last two weeks. I'll put the kettle on–

RODDY: I'll do it.

EFFIE: No, you won't–
You young people stay here and get yourselves – sorted out–

SPIKE: You just got outta the hospital–

EFFIE: Look dear, I take so many damn pills these days
I can't keep track. I probably took
too many green ones and not enough blue ones–

Effie exits.

RODDY: You must've been to the ocean by now–

SPIKE: I'm still waiting on Terry to take me there.

EFFIE: (*Offstage*) How many lumps do youse want?

SPIKE:	RODDY:
None.	One.

SPIKE:	RODDY:
None.	One.
None!	
	One!

EFFIE: (*Offstage*) All right!
One for one.
None for one.

RODDY: Spike, why do you dress like that?

SPIKE: I'm a dyke–

RODDY: Yeah–

SPIKE: A virtual dykology.
I been a bar dyke.
A dude dyke.
A birkenstock dyke.
Now I'm a bike dyke.

RODDY: Why do you have to be so blatant about it?

SPIKE: Why not? Better blatant than latent.
Two women fucking may be just a turn-on for some men but for some lesbians it means taking our own pleasure in our own hands and coming a lot.

RODDY: It's just the sex? C'mon.

SPIKE: Oh, Roddy, it's everything–
it's the way they walk, the way they talk–
the way they think.
Their stories.
Their hands. Their hearts. Their loving wise ways.
The way they make me feel.
So-o-o-o-o good.
When I was little I didn't know what a "girl" was–
I didn't know I was a girl–
Not a "boy," but not a girl either.
I was just me. A "tweensy."

Roddy laughs, understanding.

Now I feel like a whole person.
Naw, fucking is only part of it, Roddy.
The idea of women having sex in a society–
that hates sex,
and women, not to mention lesbians–
makes it dangerous.
For me. For us.
I hate the danger, but I take it on.
Because I'm a dyke.
I love women.
Does that answer your question?

RODDY: Yeah–
I think that about covers it.

SPIKE: Good.
Are you still in love with Terry?

RODDY: I'll always be in love with Terry.

SPIKE: You're not a threat.

RODDY: I don't want to be.

SPIKE: Will you talk to her?

RODDY: About–

SPIKE: About cards, letters, Frank–
did she tell you about them?

RODDY: She mentioned something–

SPIKE: I don't think they even exist.

RODDY: If she finds a card from Frank
she can prove he didn't lie?

SPIKE: I think so.
It's hard watching her go through this.
She went back to the tavern he drinks in for a week straight!
All he does is fill her head with stories–
borrows twenty bucks off her every time she sees him–
and she gives it to him!
She's really getting carried away–
I don't know what to do–

RODDY: I'll talk to her. I'll try.

SPIKE: Thanks.

RODDY: Frank changed the hearts and minds of
a lot of people before he went under–
We all loved him.
But he did go under.

SPIKE: I know.
What did Frank do?

RODDY: He stole the union's membership dues.

SPIKE: Does Terry know?

RODDY: Everybody knows.
Rita tried to keep it from her as long as possible–
I told her the night before she left Cape Breton.

Enter Effie with a plate of cookies.

EFFIE: Storeboughts! Storeboughts!
Those girls pigged out on all my homemades.

RODDY: What about those date squares?

EFFIE: Look, you little christer–
you go visit your Aunt Shirley once in a while–
maybe she'll make up some.

RODDY: I saw her last week.
She never bakes.

RITA: Never bakes!
Goin' concern, that one.
Of course, Cyril left her in good shape,
which is more than I can say for the men in this family.
Her and Rita used to step together in school.

SPIKE: Step?

RODDY: Come on, Effie.

Effie does a bit of a step dance, has to stop.

EFFIE: Oh-oh, that's enough for me!

RODDY: Where's Terry?

EFFIE: She went for a walk–
She tore that attic to bits lookin' for god knows what–

Effie looks from Roddy to Spike.

Boy, she is one popular girl!

BLACKOUT/MUSIC

SCENE FIVE

*Rita sitting in armchair onstage.
Terry walking, drinking from her flask;
she meets Roddy.*

RODDY: Boo!

TERRY: Roddy–

RODDY: I knew I'd find you here.
How's the work going?
The magazine article.

TERRY: Fine.

RODDY: If you need any help–
I could read what you have–

TERRY: There's nothing to read.

RODDY: Will the Dorchester columns help?

TERRY: Thanks for bringing them over.

RODDY: No problem.
I dropped over to the house,
saw Aunt Effie–

TERRY: How is she?

RODDY: She did a little impromptu step dance for Spike and me.

TERRY: She'll be in bed a week.

RODDY: Talked to Spike.
She's quite the little Red Emma–
better keep your eyes on her.

TERRY: You think so, huh?
So what did you two talk about?
Crazy misguided Terry?

RODDY: She's just really concerned about you–

TERRY: Spike doesn't understand–

RODDY: I think Spike knows only too well.
You're like you were six years ago–
like a sparrow–

TERRY: Pecking its way out of a cement shell.
That's exactly how it felt then
and that's exactly how I feel now–

RODDY: But you've come out since then–

TERRY: But not to my mother!
Jesus Christ, why the fuck don't you guys
have to tell your mothers you're straight?

RODDY: Want me to tell her?

TERRY: Oh, yeah, Roddy–
That would go over like a fart in church.

Since meeting Spike
I've come out more and more.
I've learned so much from her.
She's my ... ocean–
Which reminds me–
I have to take her there.

RODDY: Kennington Cove–

TERRY: She's really brave, you know–
not a chickenshit like me.

What about you?
Have you been alone all this time?

RODDY: No.

TERRY: Roddy–

RODDY: Well, yeah.

Terry comforts Roddy.

TERRY: I always felt close to you because you were the
only one who knew.
But I always wished you were a woman–

RODDY: Terry,
Spike says you're giving Frank money.

TERRY: What?
Are you two ganging up on me now or what?

RODDY: Terry,
You sound just like your father–

Stops her from leaving.

TERRY: Why would Frank steal money from his own union!

RODDY: The mortgage payments were killing him.
Terry–
I know you love Frank–
I remember he was a wonderful man.
But he cracked under the pressure–

TERRY: He wouldn't have just lied to me!
He's my father, for crissake!

RODDY: Listen, Terry,
Frank wasn't the only one destroyed
by Black Friday.
He jumped ship–
he left your mother.

TERRY: I took care of my mother!

RODDY: Everybody knows you took care of your mother
after Frank left.
But what about now?
She's so worried you're gonna end up like Frank–

TERRY: I'm not gonna end up like Frank!

Walking away.

I can't take much more of this–

RODDY: Where are you going?

TERRY: I don't know.
Somewhere.
Somewhere for a drink.

RODDY: Rita's making supper.
She'll worry.

TERRY: Let her!
She never believed in Dad.
Everything he did for this Island
means nothing to her!

RODDY: That's not true and you know it.

TERRY: She should've married Cyril!
And had boring passive children.
At least I still believe in what he tried
to do for this island,
the changes he tried to make–

RODDY: Will finding one birthday card
make this any easier for you?

TERRY: Fuck off, Roddy!

Terry runs off.

RODDY: Terry!!!

    Roddy walks back to the house. Lights up on Rita.
    Roddy enters.

RITA: What did she say?

RODDY: She still believes in Frank–

RITA: I can understand why – I did.

RODDY: He's telling her he's written to her all these years.

RITA: He didn't send her so much as a birthday card–
and she knows it!

    After he picked up and left
and the shit hit the fan, she blamed me.
Everyone looked at me out of the corner of their eye.
Fallen heroes skip town
and the poor woman is left to pick up the pieces
and all Terry could do was scream at me–
"Stop crying! He's not dead!"

    Oh, Roddy, it's happening all over again.
Her father is deserting her again.

RODDY: She has you.

RITA: Fat lot of good I am.
What if she never comes back?
Leaves for good?
She'll never give up this beautiful picture she has of Frank–
the beautiful picture I have of Frank–
the Frank who laughed–
Frank – the man with the stars in his eyes.
"Cock-of-the-walk!"
I always got a kick out of the way he walked.
A good, steady, sure walk–

    His hands were like a woman's–
Like Terry's.
He could pick up the smallest things–
I always teased him about it.
Oh, my god, Roddy–

    Roddy comforts Rita.

Enter Effie.

EFFIE: I just popped in to tell you
I called Sister Theresa.
We're gonna go to bingo as soon as she's off the crutches.

I only did it because Spike said if I didn't smarten up
She wasn't gonna take me for a spin on that bike.

*Roddy laughs. Effie exits.
Roddy and Rita look at each other.*

RITA: What did she say?

BLACKOUT/MUSIC

SCENE SIX

Later. Spike, Effie and Roddy are in the living room, sipping Cold Duck.

EFFIE: Those twins are bad!!
Last month Tiffany wrote Tammy's exam–
they're foolin' people already.
I couldn't tell one from the other when they first moved in–
they fooled me all the time–

Enter Rita.

One time they had me fooled into
thinking they were both in bed,
so Tiffany could sneak out and go to the softball game–

RITA: You take it easy on that Cold Duck, Effie.
Don't wanna have to pick you
up off the floor two nights in a row–

EFFIE: Miss Prim–

RITA: Effie, don't you start–

Where is Terry?
I been holding supper almost an hour–
Fifteen minutes and I'm dialing 911.

EFFIE: Oh, for pity's sake–
leave Terry be–
she'll be here.

RODDY: Missing your first supper home is a mortal sin in Cape Breton, right, Rita?

SPIKE: She probably just went for a drink.

RITA: See, even you're worried, aren't you, dear–
I'm callin' the police–

EFFIE: Oh, don't be so foolish!

RITA: I know my own daughter!

EFFIE: And I know mine!

RODDY: *(To Spike)* Here we go!

EFFIE: Getting her drawers in a knot for nothing!

RITA: What did you say?

EFFIE: You heard me!

RITA: You knew I knew!

SPIKE: Everybody knows!

EFFIE: His dirty old grandmother told you!

RITA: You coulda opened your mouth–

EFFIE: I just did!
You're a good one to talk!

RITA: *(To Roddy)* How many times have I held my tongue–
Papa's funeral–
Terry's first birthday–

EFFIE: All those years
you never let on you knew!

RITA: My last birthday–

EFFIE: You little christer!
I gave you that microwave!

RITA: You miserable old cow!
I wanted my mother, not some effin' microwave–

RODDY: Okay, girls–

EFFIE: Throw the damn thing out, then!

RITA: Gladly!

EFFIE: Ohh! You lay one hand on that–!

RITA: I'll do what I damn well please!

RODDY: Will you two listen to yourselves?
Going on and on about a stupid microwave–
Everybody knows!

Silence

RITA: Oh, mother–

They hug each other and bawl their eyes out.

EFFIE: Oh, honey, I been waitin' a lot of years to hear that!

RODDY: Two peas in a pod.
When I first moved here
I was told not to let on I knew–
but it was so obvious.
These two were so sweet, though–
had me over for a nice cuppa tea–
Remember, Effie, I had a pony tail back then.
Everyone teased me about it
but not these two–

EFFIE: He looked like Jesus H. Christ himself!
Never washed.
Who's cuttin' your hair now, Roddy?
Helen Keller?

RODDY: You're cut off.

EFFIE: Ahh, Roddy.
You know the women in this family
never did have much sense–
fallin' for drifters and drunkards and dreamers and–

Glances at Spike.

This family coulda used a man like you–
Trouble is you were just too damn normal!

SPIKE: Well, seeing as this is turning into a coming-out party–

RITA: What was that, dear?

SPIKE: When I first came out–

EFFIE: Came out where, dear?

SPIKE: Out–
Out of the closet–

EFFIE: RITA:
Oh!   Oh!

SPIKE: My girlfriend and I were in the bathtub fooling around–
havin' a ball–
everybody was out working, we made sure of that.
I'm fourteen, she's fifteen.
We're up to our ass in Mr. Bubbles.
Our hands are all over each other.
We're getting so carried away,
we don't know what to touch next or how.
Then, the door flies open–
my sister–
who's in my girlfriend's class–

I've never heard anyone scream that loud before
or since – except you, Aunt Effie.

Well, she didn't waste any time
telling our mother
or the whole school for that matter.

Biggest favour my sister ever did for me.

Effie laughs, catches herself.

RITA: Spike–
Is Terry gay – or happy – or whatever it is they call it?

SPIKE: Well, Rita, that's something
you'll have to ask Terry yourself–

Rita looks to Effie and Roddy. They are no help.

RITA: I knew something was up
when she started hanging out with that Gosby girl–
I always warned her about girls like Kathy Gosby.
She was a bad one, let me tell ya–
smokin' and drinkin'
from the age of twelve.
Caught her smokin' a cigar once–

EFFIE: Scalloped potatoes are probably gone to mush by now–

RITA:	Lord above–
	if it's not one thing it's the other–
	I don't know what's going on in my own house anymore–
EFFIE:	Papa left this house to me, remember!
RITA:	Oh, for crissake Effie!

Terry bursts into the room.

TERRY:	Will you two give it a rest!
	Everybody just shut up and listen!
	Ma – meet your mother!
RITA:	Terry–
TERRY:	Ma, she knows you know she's your daughter.
	Tell her, Gramma–
EFFIE:	Well, dear, we–
TERRY:	You and Ma mean more to me than anything
	and if you don't stop fighting like cats and dogs
	I'm gonna lose my mind!
RODDY:	Terry,
	Effie and Rita–
TERRY:	As for Dad–
	I knew he was lying–
	I probably knew it all along–
	But he's my father for crissake!
	I had to try!
RITA:	Yes, dear, we–
TERRY:	Look at Gandhi!
	Treated his wife and kids like shit!
	Does anyone remember? No-o-o-o.
	So why does Dad have to be remembered for his mistakes?
	After everything he did for this island–
	it's not fair!
RITA:	Terry, your supper's–
TERRY:	People can only take so much.
	What happened on Black Friday was Dad's last straw–
	he gave up trying to change things.
	And who could blame him?

A lot of good ones go under–
and that's what pisses me off–
but there's always another good one on the way.
Someone passionate.
Someone who gives a fuck – excuse me, Ma–
someone just like Dad.
I know Dad lied to me
but he lied to himself too–
I know now you only get stronger when you tell the truth.

I feel like a groundhog–
have ever since I got here–
wondering whether it's safe to come out–
afraid of my own shadow.

Here I thought I'd been coming out all my life–
but what do I do?
I spend my Christmases with "friends"
because I can't bring my lover home.

Ma–
Gramma–
Roddy–
This is who I spent last Christmas with.

We live together.
We shop together.
We walk down the street holding hands.

Now I would love to be private
but for some of us
being private is a luxury we can't afford.
We have to be public first.
And the day I stop coming out is the day I check out.
I hate to kiss in public but I do it!

Yes, Ma, I kiss Spike in public!
Spike, kiss me now, in public!

SPIKE: Terry, I think you should sit down.

Terry sits.

TERRY: Thank you.

EFFIE: Supper ready yet? I'm starving!

Effie exits.

RITA: Spikey dear, help Roddy set the table.

Spike and Roddy exit, Rita sits in front of Terry, lifts her chin and looks her daughter in the eye.

RITA: Welcome to Cape Breton, dear.

TERRY: Ma!

They hug.

BLACKOUT/MUSIC
"Jack to the Sound of the Underground" by Hithouse.

♦♦♦

Acknowledgements

Audrey would like to thank the following individuals and organizations for their advice, encouragement, support and inspiration: Kate Johnston, Marguerite McNeil, Marcia Johnson, Merle Matheson, Grant Carmichael, Marie Bridget Dundon, Bryden MacDonald, Christine Plunkett, Veronica Macdonald, Tracey Izatt, Hugo Dann, Larry Fineberg, Carol Bolt, Libby Bradburne, The Lesbian and Gay Community Appeal of Toronto, Maria Crawford, Sky Gilbert, Tim Jones, Sue Golding, Buddies in Bad Times Theatre, Grant Ramsay, Kate Lushington, Nightwood Theatre, Jim Millan, Company of Sirens, Cynthia Grant, Colleen Moore, Ontario Arts Council, Ground Level Graphics, Shaw Festival, Canadian Stage, Tarragon Theatre, Canada Council, Ellen Pierce, Tomson Highway, Ruthann Tucker, Dougal Newport, Tannis Atkinson, Beth Walden, Sunday Harrison, Marcy Rogers, Jennifer Ross, Gregory Nixon, David Ramsden, *Rites* Magazine, Michael Fitzgerald, Duncan & Theresa, Roy Butler, Cathy Theriault, Dimanche, Mary Theresa Lawlor, Leslie Spit Tree-o, Theatrum, Denise Benson, Bathurst Street Peace and Justice Centre, Pink Antenna, Canadian Actors' Equity Association, Madonna, Elvis and the Virgin Mary.

CLAPOSIS

Overleaf: L. to R.
Shelley Ledger as "Kate"
Ellen-Ray Hennesey as "Judy"
Siobhan McCormick as "Beth"

PHOTOS BY DONNA MARCHAND

Playwright's Note

Pulling myself together to direct a remount of this play in the Fringe of Toronto Festival 1990, I think back to the original *Claposis* produced six years ago. Once again it was the generosity, talent and energy of the people involved in both productions that got me through. I'd never had a play produced that wasn't designed, directed, cast and written by myself. I'd never had a play produced in Toronto, or any other major city for that matter. I'd never written about being a dyke before. I was scared shitless and exhilarated at the same time.

The first read-through of the first draft: not pretty. But the actors gave their all and I saw where it could go. Rewrites were in order, of course. A writer is only as good as her rewrites, I always say. It got better, much better, quickly. Pretty soon we had a hit on our hands. We managed to scrape the money together and hold the production over for a week.

Writing *Claposis* was one of the best experiences of my life. I learned, I laughed, I clapped, I fell in love, I met a lot of fun, crazy, wonderful people, on stage and off. That's what theatre's all about, isn't it?

Audrey Butler
4:30 a.m., May 24, 1990
Toronto

Director's Note

I've often been asked if this production of *Claposis* would be politically correct. I don't know if it is or not. It seems, though, that political correctness is something a director is supposed to be aware of when working with gay themes, particularly if the characters are lesbians. I must admit that one of the qualities I found especially attractive about *Claposis* was that it didn't seem to care whether or not it was correct. It is not propaganda. It is not self-conscious. It is simply a play about three people trying to solve their problems. After all, lying beneath all those political causes are emotions and human nature. That is what *Claposis* is about. Am I correct?

Robert Scott
August 1985
Toronto

PRODUCTION NOTES

The first production of *Claposis* was a workshop produced by Gemini Theatre, Toronto, and performed in the backspace of Theatre Passe Muraille in August 1985. It was directed by Robert Scott and designed by the company. The cast was as follows:

JUDY	....	Ellen Ray Hennessy
KATE	....	Shelley Ledger
BETH	....	Siobhan McCormick

A second production was one of the four plays in Buddies in Bad Times Theatre's first 4-Play Festival of Lesbian and Gay Works, December 1985. It was also directed by Robert Scott, with the original cast, at the Backspace of Theatre Passe Muraille, Toronto, December 1985.

♦♦♦

CLAPOSIS

A one-act play in eleven scenes, arranged in reverse chronological order.

No intermission.

Set in the back room of Claposis, a new-age vintage clothing store on Queen Street West, Toronto, or in a giant bed with a mannequin, a bird cage, a French stick, tea cups, wine glasses, and lots of blankets and pillows.

Music during blackouts: Operatic selections by Teresa Berganza, Decca Records, London.

CAST OF CHARACTERS

KATE   Owner of "Claposis," a new-age vintage clothing store on Queen Street West, Toronto. Down to earth.

JUDY   Aspiring playwright.
A ferris wheel on legs,
trying hard not to grow up.

BETH   Aspiring poet and wild dresser, "trendy femme" sophisticate.

SCENE ONE

*Back room of Claposis,
late one early summer evening.
Music ends, door slams, all three enter.*

JUDY: Hiya there, Katie.
Thought we'd drop in,
see how you're doin'.
Busy?

KATE: I just made a pot of tea.
Would you like some?

Exits to offstage kitchen

JUDY: Yeah, sure.
What about you, Beth?

Beth!

BETH: *(whipping off walkman headphones)*
Wha–?

JUDY: You wanna cuppa tea?

BETH: Yeah, sure. Great.

Pause

JUDY: *(notices missing bird cage)*
Kate!
Where are–
What happened to the birds, Kate?
You didn't–

Kate enters

You didn't give them away, did you?

KATE: No.
They died.

Kate exits

JUDY: So why didn't you call me?
Huh?

BETH: Judy–

JUDY: Well, she coulda called me.

Kate enters.

KATE: I did, but you were never home.

JUDY: You coulda called me at Beth's.

KATE: It never crossed my mind.
Pause
I'll get the tea.
Exits

BETH: What a tacky thing to say.
Kate enters.

KATE: All I have is honey.

BETH: Honey's great! Love honey.
It's so-o-o-o good for you.
Here, have a cuppa tea.
All sip tea.

JUDY: So when did the little poopers croak?

KATE: A couple of weeks ago.

JUDY: The male was sick last time I was here.

BETH: Maybe they were sick when you bought 'em.
A friend of mine–

JUDY: Hey, yeah.
We were always wonderin'
why they never made any noise–
bird sounds or whatever–

BETH: When Jeff's parrot died
he had an autopsy done,
got his money back.

JUDY: He would.
Kate doesn't wanna do that though,
do you, Kate?

KATE: That would be difficult.
I didn't keep their little carcasses.
All sip, loudly.

CLAPOSIS / 73

              So.
              Where you two coming from?
JUDY: You tell her,
              it was your idea.
BETH: Oh, tell her yourself.
JUDY: We were fighting on our way here.
BETH: We were not fighting.
JUDY: Oh, sorry,
              we were having a difference of opinion–
              all because of this stupid
              "playreading series"–
BETH: Oh, come on,
              it wasn't that bad–
JUDY: Yeah, right.
              The one about the cat named Snowball
              was pretty powerful.
KATE: Snowball?
BETH: See?
              Where's your sense of humour?
              You'd think theatre was
              something sacred.
JUDY: Well, it used to be.
BETH: When was the last time
              you had a play produced?
JUDY: When was the last time
              you had a poem published?
                         Pause
KATE: How is the writing going?
JUDY: Great! I'm up to five lines.
KATE: A minute?
JUDY: A week.

	Beth here might have a job, though. In a publishing house, no less.
KATE:	That's great, Beth. You must be pleased.
BETH:	Probably just a glorified go-for by the sound of it–
KATE:	Still, it's what you've been looking for, isn't it? Publishing, I mean–
JUDY:	Wait till you hear what she did–
BETH:	Judy–
JUDY:	Tell Kate what you did.
BETH:	I lit up a cigarette just before the interview.
JUDY:	After I told her not to–
BETH:	It was the principle of the thing–
JUDY:	Really? I thought it was because you were nervous–
BETH:	I was. But I'll be really pissed off if I don't get the job because of that. You're so lucky you have Cape–
KATE & JUDY:	Claposis.
BETH:	Claposis.
JUDY:	How's business?
KATE:	Great. New owners are tearing down the building next week.
BETH:	Oh, no.
KATE:	I'm just in the middle of packing–

BETH: What are you gonna do?

JUDY: What if somebody has to get in touch with you?

KATE: A friend of mine asked me to
manage one of her stores.

JUDY: Diane!

KATE: Call her office if you want.

JUDY: I'd have a better chance with the PTL Club—

BETH: That's great.
I mean,
you're not destitute or anything—

JUDY: Are you moving in with her too?
Have you ever been to one of Diane's stores?
I don't know where she gets her stock
but I wouldn't wear it to the laundromat.

KATE: Remember all those belts I made,
like the one I made for you?
Well, I sold them all.
And Diane—tacky, tasteless Diane—
wants more.
They're selling out at Chic.

BETH: Chic? Your lover owns the Chic line?
Oh, wow.
The clothes there are gorgeous.
A friend of a friend of a friend of mine
can actually afford to buy clothes there—

JUDY: Beth.

BETH: What?

JUDY: Finished your tea yet?

BETH: Why?

JUDY: I think we should leave.
Let Kate get packing.

Judy and Beth get ready to leave.

KATE: Well,
I'm really glad you two
dropped by.

BETH: It was nice seeing you again.
I'm really sorry about Claposis.

KATE: Come by Saturday.
I'm having a going-out-of-business sale.

BETH: Thanks.

JUDY: I'll see you outside, okay?

BETH: I think I'll go straight home.

JUDY: Beth–

BETH: I'll call you next week.
If I'm not too busy.
Bye!

Beth exits

JUDY: Beth!
Geezhowdoyoulikethat!

KATE: You shouldn't've brought her here–

JUDY: I couldn't help myself,
I had to see you.

KATE: Judy–

JUDY: Here, I'll help you pack–

KATE: Judy!

JUDY: I helped you move in. Remember?

KATE: I think you should leave
while you can still walk.
Maybe you could still
catch up with Beth–

JUDY: Kate! She's pissed off!

KATE: I'm sure you'll think of something
to make it up to her.

JUDY: Coupla orgasms, she'll be fine.
Whadda ya want me to do?
Go crawlin' after her?
Beth!
Come back to me, Beth!
I'm nothing without you.
You're nothing without me–
We should be joined at the hip!

> *Judy burps, falls flat on her ass.*
> *Kate helps her up.*

I think I drank too much.

> *Kisses Kate.*

KATE: Judy ... please,
all I want is friendship.

> *Pause.*
> *Judy stomps out, door slams.*

Bye.

BLACKOUT/MUSIC

SCENE TWO

> *Back room of Claposis, late spring,*
> *late evening. Bird cage is back.*
> *Judy and Kate enter.*

JUDY: Fuuuckk!
Whadda dumb movie.
Shoulda shot the director instead.
Way Fonda was holdin' that cigarette–
Whadda retard!

Never mind. Ya had to be there.
What's wrong?

KATE: The birds are sick.

JUDY: Maybe they're just tired.

KATE: They haven't sung a note for days.

JUDY: Take 'em to the vet.
I'll take 'em to the vet.

What else?

KATE: And.

JUDY: And.

KATE: I want this to stop.
I want it to stop right now.

JUDY: What?

Oh.
I'll leave, then.
I knew it was stupid
to invite myself back here–

Can't we spend one more night together?

Kate shakes her head

You really want me to go?

*Kate nods. Judy moves to leave.
Kate throws her arms around Judy.*

KATE: Sometimes it feels like
I can't breathe–
live another moment without you.

JUDY: Yeah?

KATE: Look at me!
I must be losing my mind.

JUDY: What's wrong with that?

KATE: We have to start
taking this seriously, Judy.

JUDY: Oh, for god's sake.
Sound like a fucking
camp counsellor–

KATE: Can't you say anything without using that word?

JUDY: What, camp?

KATE: There are more important things in life
than "fucking"–

JUDY: Wheewww!!!

KATE: I bet you haven't
written a word
since we met,
have you.

JUDY: You've got nothing to do
with me not writing.
I know what this is all about:
Why did you say you weren't upset
when I slept with Beth
after you asked me not to
if you were?

KATE: I shouldn't've asked you
to begin with.
You should sleep with other people–

JUDY: Now I'm completely confused–

KATE: I was using you.

JUDY: I know.
Why stop now?
A man?
Another woman?
Your career?
What?

KATE: Not a man.
Diane.
She offered me a job.
I'll have to take it,
even if I don't lose the store.
So I'll be too busy
to see you
anyway.

JUDY: You don't even respect Diane.
How could you even think about going back?
You know what she's like:
it'll be like being back in the closet–

KATE: She promised it would be different.

JUDY: Fine.

> *Judy stomps out, re-enters.*

Don't forget to call the "fucking" pet store.

> *Kate throws a styrofoam wig head at her.*

BLACKOUT/MUSIC

SCENE THREE

Back room of Claposis, mid-spring, early evening. Kate and Judy in bed reading a letter.

JUDY: When did this come?

KATE: This morning.

JUDY: Oh, fuck.

KATE: Beth'll be here any minute. You better get ready.

JUDY: You wanna come with us? I'm sure Beth wouldn't mind.

KATE: I think I'll stay here.

JUDY: Chant–

KATE: Meditate–

JUDY: Line up the crystals–

> *They neck. Door bangs shut. They jump up. Judy exits. Beth enters*

BETH: Hi. How was your ... dinner.

KATE: Nothing special. How's the job hunting going?

BETH: It's not.
Actually, I'm taking a couple of weeks off
to recuperate from the one I just had.
I don't want to wait on another table
for as long as I live.

KATE: What are you looking for?

BETH: Something in publishing–
So it's probably hopeless.
Judy's here, isn't she?

Judy pops in.

JUDY: Hi, Bethyboo!!

Beth waves. Judy pops out.

BETH: Or worse:
I could end up back at my old job.

KATE: How long did you work there?

BETH: Two years.

KATE: You think they fired you because you were gay?

BETH: Well, I wasn't fired exactly.

KATE: Oh.

BETH: And I wasn't out exactly.
Judy's right:
I should've opened my mouth
as soon as it started–
insinuations, remarks–
put them in their place.
I'm no good at that, though.
Look where being wimpy got me.
Maybe it's time I got political too.

KATE: Judy? Political?

BETH: Well, she is pretty out.
Isn't that enough these days?
She's gonna be late, too.

KATE: Do you read first?

Beth starts to pace.

BETH: No, third.
But I'd like to hear the others.

KATE: I don't think that'll be any problem.
It's only a two-minute walk.

BETH: Further west, isn't it?
It's not that close, is it?

KATE: Are you nervous?

Beth shakes her head, then nods.

Have you ever read in public before?

Beth nods, then shakes her head.

I'm sure everything'll be just fine.

BETH: Are you coming with us?

KATE: I have to do some work.
But I'd really love to read
some of your poems sometime.
Judy really thinks a lot of
your work.

BETH: She does?

KATE: I'm sure she won't be a minute–
But then again–

BETH: Oh, I know–
Has she ever met you on time
for anything?

KATE: She certainly has a charming way
of making up for it–

Judy enters.

JUDY: Do do do do do do da!!!

KATE: Well, it's about time.

JUDY: We're not gonna be late, are we?

*Judy rushes around
getting ready to leave.*

	What were you two gals talking about? Huh?
BETH:	Work.
JUDY:	Oh. Did Kate show you that awful letter?
BETH:	What letter?
KATE:	Oh, it's nothing.
JUDY:	Kate.
KATE:	I got a notice saying the owners have sold the building–
JUDY:	You could lose Claposis, Kate.
BETH:	Oh, Kate, why didn't you say something? Here I was going on and on about my own problems–
KATE:	You're both gonna be late.
BETH:	I think she should come with us.
KATE:	I'm fine. I'm not gonna do anything drastic.
JUDY:	Oh oh. Drastic? You? Maybe you better come with us.
KATE:	I'll be fine!
JUDY:	She'll be fine. Just gotta line up your crystals or something, right?
KATE:	Right. Good luck on your reading. *(To Judy)* I'll call you tomorrow, okay? Bye.

> *Beth and Judy exit.*
> *Kate crosses to phone.*

Diane Diane Diane.

>   *Dials phone. Hangs up*

Not Diane.
Judy.
Leave a message on her machine.
>   *Dials and listens.*

Tell her
I never want to see her again.
Well, once in a while–
To have sex–
You have to get your life together–
So do I–
That's what I said last time–
Which lasted till I came back from Montreal
a week later.
I'll bury myself in work–
encourage her to do–
>   *Hangs up.*

Damn!
She hasn't put her machine on
since the last time we broke up.
Listen to yourself–
Talkin' to myself till I'm blue in the face–
Why shouldn't I do something drastic?
>   *Pause*

I'll write her a note–
>   *Finds neither pen nor paper.*

Can't even write her a note!
My crystals must be
really outta whack–
>   *Closes her eyes, takes a deep breath.*

Think about...
Standing on the edge of
the Atlantic.
Aunt Mamie's Las Vegas cigarettes–
all different pastel colours
with gold tips–
I went down to the shore
and smoked every one of them–

Sat there for hours
listening to the ocean–
Waves sucking me in
rocks rumbling
spray soaking–
wondering what to do with my life–
watching the sun come up:
"rosy fingers of dawn"
over the ocean
she talked to you with her waves–
Now she wants to swallow you whole!
She does!

Pause

You probably think
I'm really ... flaky
or something.
People've said it before.
What if I am!

I need more time!

Phone rings.

Hello?

Oh, hi.
It's you.
I thought it might be Diane–
Did you forget something?

I'm fine.

Listen, Judy, I'm glad you called–

Okay, okay.
Call me when you get home.

I'll talk to you then.

Yes.

I love you too.

Hangs up.

If I don't
do something
soon
I'm gonna drown!

Jumps up.
Don't do anything drastic.
Feed the birds
and don't do anything drastic.
    Feeds the birds.

BLACKOUT/MUSIC

SCENE FOUR

Back room of Claposis. Judy and Beth. Judy is making faces at the birds.

JUDY: They never make any noise.
They don't like me.

BETH: You're supposed to make noises,
not faces, at them–

    Beth demonstrates.

JUDY: Ha ha ha–
They don't like you either.

BETH: How long you doing this for?

JUDY: Coupla days.
Until Kate gets back from Montreal.

BETH: What about the restaurant?

JUDY: I had a coupla days coming to me.

BETH: What's she doing there?
Why didn't you go with her?

JUDY: Fashion show/convention or something.

BETH: Must be nice.

JUDY: She goes every year with Diane.

BETH: Diane?

JUDY: Her ex.

BETH: Oh.
Is that why you called me?

JUDY: No!
I wanted to see you.
This place is driving me up the wall.
All I do all day is drink wine
and play with myself.

BETH: Doesn't anyone ever come in?

JUDY: Hardly ever.

BETH: *(Offering a cigarette)* Want one?

JUDY: Thanks.
Yesterday some nut came in
and demanded I change the name
of the store!

BETH: What?

JUDY: Kept going on and on about Armageddon–

BETH: How'd you get rid of him?

JUDY: Bought one of his stupid pamphlets–
can you believe it?

BETH: Well, I'm not too crazy
about the name myself–
an oceanographic term for two waves meeting–
Kate has a bad case of symbolism, if you ask me.

JUDY: You're just jealous
'cause you didn't think of it first.
So am I.

Gettin' much work done on your poems?

BETH: No.

JUDY: Why not?

BETH: I don't know.
I just can't seem to do much
of anything
these days.

JUDY: Maybe you're trying too hard.

BETH: I'm not trying at all.

JUDY: You got that reading coming up–

BETH: I can't even decide what to read.

JUDY: Read some of them to me–
especially the one about the legs–

BETH: Let me shave them!

JUDY: What, my legs?

BETH: No, your feet, stupid.

JUDY: I'm closin' up in fifteen minutes.

BETH: Maybe we should go out.

JUDY: What for?
C'mere, droopy drawers.
What's wrong?

BETH: I don't know.
All I do is think about you.
About being with you.

JUDY: Well, you're with me now, ain'tcha?

BETH: I was hurt when you told me
Kate didn't want us sleeping together–
I know she's in love with you–
Are you in love with Kate?

JUDY: Unfortunately.

BETH: Why?
I think it's wonderful!
Just what you've always wanted.
You're not in love with me, are you?

JUDY: No.

BETH: Good.
I told you
I can't give you what Kate gives you–

	All we have is a physical relationship– Or used to.
JUDY:	We still can–
BETH:	What about Kate?
JUDY:	I don't know– I hope you don't think I rejected you– I mean, I'm not in love with you but– Oh god, I don't know what I mean– What am I gonna do?
BETH:	Maybe I should leave.
JUDY:	Okay.
BETH:	Before something happens.
JUDY:	Whadda ya think's gonna happen?

They look at the bed between them.

	Kate and I aren't seeing each other anymore.
BETH:	Isn't she supposed to be in love with you?
JUDY:	We've broken up three times in the last two weeks. Look at me! I'm a mess!
BETH:	You think it's because of me–
JUDY:	Because of you what?
BETH:	That you and Kate are having these problems because of me?
JUDY:	Naa!! I think she's really scared. No matter what happens– Don't ever think that.
BETH:	So what's your official status now?
JUDY:	Friends.

BETH: Well, that's probably what she needs
more than anything right now.

JUDY: What about me?
I wanna make love with her.
With you.

> *Turns to Betty the mannequin.*

With you!

BETH: Just because Kate's not here.

JUDY: No!
I know that's the way it sounds,
but no.
Believe me?
What about you?
Have you heard from Faith lately?

BETH: Just that letter I told you about.

JUDY: The one you got after you lost your job?
Answer it yet?

BETH: Don't know what to say.

JUDY: Tell her to stop writing you.
That's all you have to say.
You don't owe her anything.

BETH: It's not that simple.
I know she loves me.

JUDY: Oh, and I don't?
Or do I?

BETH: You told me you loved Kate–

JUDY: Well maybe, just maybe,
I got this thing for you too, okay!
Okay?

> *They kiss.*

Ummm, tastes...
tastes just like apples.

Laughter

BLACKOUT/MUSIC

SCENE FIVE

Kate in the back room of Claposis, working. Judy in her apartment, picks up the phone, dials. Phone rings in back room.

KATE: Hello.

JUDY: Hi.

KATE: Oh, hi.
How are you?

JUDY: Fine.
I just got your message.
So-o-o-o.
I guess the "on-again/off-again romance" is off again, huh?

KATE: Are you okay?

JUDY: Yeah.
I'm just dandy.
Just thought I'd call,
let you know I got it.

KATE: You feel okay?
About us?

JUDY: Yeah.
I'll miss you.
But you're right.
You've got your work to do,
I've got mine.

KATE: We'll see each other again.

JUDY: Yeah, well–
I guess I better let you go–

KATE: You take care.

JUDY: I will. You too.
Bye!

> *They hang up. Judy attacks her receiver, dials again Phone rings in backroom*

KATE: Hello.

JUDY: Hi, honey.
It's me again.
You still want me to run
the store for you
while you're in Montreal?

KATE: I could get someone else–

JUDY: I'll do it!
It's not a problem for me.
Is it a problem for you?

KATE: I just don't want to take advantage of you–

JUDY: That's not a problem.

KATE: Judy–

JUDY: I'd be really hurt if you didn't want me–

KATE: Okay, okay.

JUDY: Great!

KATE: See you on Thursday, then.

JUDY: Oh, goody. Bye.

> *Both hang up.*

BLACKOUT/MUSIC

SCENE SIX

Back room of Claposis.
KATE and JUDY in bed, under a sheet.

KATE: Judy! For godsake!
You're driving me crazy!
We're both gonna die tomorrow
if we don't get some sleep.

JUDY: Can't I even touch you afterwards?

KATE: Yes.
Just don't touch me there.

JUDY: Where? Here?

> *They wrestle. Kate pins Judy.*

KATE: Judy!
We both have to work tomorrow.

Now close your eyes.
Close your eyes.
I've got a surprise for you.

> *Kate buzzes her on the neck.*
> *More horseplay.*

JUDY: Tell me something–

KATE: What?

JUDY: Ain't I just the best schtupp-mate
you've ever had?

KATE: One of the best.

JUDY: One of many?

KATE: Aren't I?

JUDY: I just wanted to impress you
when we first started schtuppin'–

KATE: Well, you certainly did.

JUDY: I was braggin' then–
I feel really stupid.
I thought I might've...

	hurt your feelings. I don't know.
KATE:	What are you trying to say?
JUDY:	What is it between us?
KATE:	Well, we have a lot of fun together. You make me laugh.
JUDY:	Is that it? Does that mean ... you don't feel anything for me?
KATE:	Of course not. Of course I do.

Pulls Judy down on top of her.

Every time you touch me.

They kiss.

JUDY:	Kate. Are you in love with me?
KATE:	What do you think I'm trying to say?

Pause

JUDY:	Ohhh!!! Why is life so fucked up! Sorry.
KATE:	Why? Because of Beth? I know you love her. And I don't care how many times she denies it, I know she loves you too.
JUDY:	Beth and I are just friends. That's all. Just friends. You and I are lovers.
KATE:	You sleep together.
JUDY:	Is that it? I won't if you don't want me to.

KATE: Judy!
It shouldn't be something I want.
Besides, you should be with Beth.
She needs you more than I do.

JUDY: Want me to go over to her apartment right now?

KATE: No, no, no.

JUDY: Now I'm confused–

KATE: It's just that sometimes...
I can't bear the thought
of you with anybody else.

JUDY: I'll stop, then.

KATE: No.
You shouldn't stop sleeping with her
because of me–

JUDY: But you're the one who brought it up.

KATE: Ohh!!
I don't care!
Sleep with her if you want.
Just don't tell me about it!

Yanks sheet over her head.

JUDY: I won't sleep with Beth anymore, okay?

Pause

Whadda ya want from me?

KATE: Right now I just want to go to sleep.

Judy climbs on top of her.

JUDY: Ummm, I love you.

BLACKOUT/MUSIC

SCENE SEVEN

*Judy in the back room of
Claposis on the phone.
Beth on the phone in her apartment.*

JUDY: Listen,
a person doesn't *catch* a yeast infection.

BETH: What causes it, then?

JUDY: Stress. Heat.
Polyester underwear.
French sticks.

BETH: Ohhh!!
What should I do about it?

JUDY: Yogurt's good.
Just put it right on your apple strudel.

BETH: Ohhh!!!
Couldn't I just eat it?

JUDY: It might do some good–

Starts to howl.

BETH: What is it?
What's so funny?

JUDY: Last summer
I had this really bad infection
and Robert–
we were still roommates then–
came home one weekend from Shaw.
The first thing he did was go to the fridge
and ask if there was any food.
I said there's yogurt
but don't eat it,
I'm using it on my cunt!

BETH: That's really disgusting!

JUDY: So I'm a pig!
What can I say!
Oh, don't be so squeamish–

	So, whadda ya think of Kate?
BETH:	She's gorgeous.
JUDY:	I know. I think I'm falling in love.
BETH:	You're always falling in love.
JUDY:	I know, but this is different. I'm trying hard not to, I really am. We've been seeing each other for almost two months. I fell in love with you the second night we slept together– boy, was I a mess.
BETH:	You were lonely, that's all it was.
JUDY:	That was not all it was– anyway, I'm glad you talked some sense into me– you coulda freaked out–
BETH:	You were good in bed– that's the only thing that saved you, baby.
JUDY:	Oh, honey, I miss you. I really need someone to talk some sense into me–
BETH:	We'll see each other soon–
JUDY:	No, tonight I mean.
BETH:	Well, I was just going out to dinner–
JUDY:	Oh. Anybody I know?
BETH:	Sort of.
JUDY:	So what's the big mystery, Bethie?
BETH:	I'm meeting Jeff.
JUDY:	Oh.

	I thought you said he was a jerk. The biggest asshole in the province.
BETH:	Judy, I've known Jeff a long time. Besides, you still see Robert–
JUDY:	True. But Robert and I were never schtupp-buddies–
BETH:	Stoop what?
JUDY:	Not stoop–schtupp– new word I heard at work. It's Yiddish for–
BETH:	I can guess what it's Yiddish for–
JUDY:	Anyway, Robert and I never schtupped– Nor is Robert an asshole–
BETH:	You'd think Robert was god the way you talked–
JUDY:	Beth, Robert happens to be my best friend–
BETH:	Well, Jeff used to be mine.
JUDY:	Okay, okay. You gonna spend the whole night with him?
BETH:	No.
JUDY:	So why can't you meet me later?
BETH:	Judy–
JUDY:	It won't be that late, will it? You could call me, but try the store– Claposis– first, that's where I am now.
BETH:	Oh–
JUDY:	Kate's gone to the O'Keefe with somebody– I'll be home later–
BETH:	I don't know how late I'll be–

JUDY: You're just going for dinner–

BETH: We might go dancing–

JUDY: Ohhhh!!! Dancing too.
Why don't you just fuck him for old times' sake while you're at it?

BETH: I might just do that–

JUDY: Fine!

Slamming the receiver a few times.

Finefinefinefine.
Fine.

BETH: *(Leaving her apartment)* Fucking bitch!

Beth exits.

JUDY: *(To mannequin)* Some friend she turned out to be, huh?
What about you, huh?
Wanna talk some sense into me?
Better off talking to myself.
Ewwww!!!
I know what I'll do!
Go to the Chez
and sweet-talk some young twatburger
into going home with me!
Yeah!
Shit!
That's probably where she'll end up with Jeffy.
Fuck! Whadda pervert!
They're both perverts
if you ask me.
"If I were the king of the for-r-r-res-st-t-t!!!"
Maybe I should wait here for Kate.
Maybe I should go home and write.
About what?
All I think about is schtuppin'.
That's because where I come from
they don't have lesbians.
Christ!
They just got cable TV!
Would you believe there was a time
when I thought more about getting cable TV
than I did about getting laid.

God, you'd think I discovered it.
When all schtuppin' is–
well, it's a lot like TV, actually.
I used to fall asleep with the TV on
now I can't fall asleep unless I'm with someone.
Weird.
Before I got my own TV
I was an insomniac–
that's why I started writing–
Not on paper at first – just in my head,
tryin' to put myself to sleep.
Now I'm a writer because...
I'm a writer! Ha!
God, what's happening to me?
Why can't I write anymore?

Spilling wine.

Why can't I pour?
Maybe you don't have anything to say.
Maybe you never did.
Never will.
Maybe that's why
you're so fucking scared.

Phone rings.

Hello?
Who the fuck is this?
Beth! You pervert!

Pause

I'm sorry too.
Want me to pick up some yogurt?
I'll put it on you personally if you want.
I'm just kidding!
Okay. See ya later. Bye.

Smooches into the phone.
Hangs up, crosses to mannequin.

What about you, huh?
Ever had a yeast infection?

Scratches mannequin's crotch

BLACKOUT/MUSIC

SCENE EIGHT

Judy in back room of Claposis singing to birds.

JUDY: Yel-l-l-l-low bird,
high up in banana tree,
Yel-l-l-l-low bird,
you sit all alone like me–

Door slams.

Whee!
Mommy's home! Mommy!

Kate enters with groceries.

KATE: Ohhh!!!
It's freezing out there!

JUDY: Here, sweetie.
Let me warm you up!

*They embrace. Beth enters.
Kate sees her, pushes Judy away*

Oh! Hi, Bethie!

Pause

Beth, Kate. Kate, Beth.

Pause

So-o-o-o-o.
Why don't I leave you two to get re-acquainted.

Judy exits to kitchen.

KATE: Judy!
So!
You're early!
Dinner'll be ready, oh...
in an hour or so.
So, Judy tells me we have something in common.

BETH: Besides her?

JUDY: *(Offstage)* Didn't you both go to King's?

KATE: Did you–

Beth nods.

	Interesting–
JUDY:	Kate!
KATE:	When did you graduate?
BETH:	I didn't. I quit in my second year.
JUDY:	Kate!
KATE:	What, honey?

Judy enters with bottle of wine.

JUDY:	Where's the corkscrew?
KATE:	Oh, in there somewhere.

Judy exits.

That's probably why
I don't remember seeing you.

BETH:	That's okay. I don't remember seeing you either– Oh, wait a minute– You were homecoming queen one year weren't you?
KATE:	Oh, my god, yes! Everyone knew me as Kathy back then. And boy was I ever a Kathy–
BETH:	Then you must remember Faith– Faith Rankin–
KATE:	Faith Rankin?
BETH:	President of the student council–
KATE:	Ohhh, yes. She was from–
BETH:	Cape Breton–

Judy enters with wine.

JUDY:	What about where I'm from?
BETH:	Kate knew Faith at King's.

KATE: Not well by any means.

JUDY: Her and Beth used to schtupp–

BETH: We were roommates.

KATE: Did you know her, Judy?

JUDY: Probably went to school with her cousins.

KATE: Umm. Well, here's to a small world–

All drink a toast.

JUDY: So what's for dinner?

KATE: Seafood chowder.

JUDY: With live sex food?

Beth laughs.

KATE: Live what?

BETH: Shrimp.
Last time Judy and I did acid
we stayed home and ordered out for shrimp–

JUDY: Live sex food–
they fuck right on your plate.
Tea biscuits!
Want me to make some?

KATE: Oh, sure–wait,
I don't have any flour.

BETH: I could go get a bag–

KATE: Don't go to all that trouble–
I did buy a French stick–

Kate exits to kitchen.

JUDY: A what?

Kate enters with French stick.

KATE: Whadda ya call this?

JUDY: French tickler!

BETH: Judy!

KATE: She doesn't know the difference–
JUDY: I do so!

> *Beth deep-throats the French stick.*

Gimme that!
Is it settled?
Do I go for flour
and give the French tickler
to Beth to take home
or what?

BETH: The French stick'll be fine.

> *Judy exits.*

KATE: Have you heard from Faith
since university?

BETH: Off and on.

> *Pause*

You're lucky to have your own store and everything–
You made most of the clothes yourself?

KATE: Some.
Others are here on consignment–
Most are second-hand, though.

> *Judy enters.*

BETH: Do you actually tell people that story
about your ex-lover
when they ask you what claposis means?

> *Judy tries to signal to Beth.*

KATE: Ex-lover?

> *Beth notices Judy.*

BETH: Yeah–

JUDY: I told Beth
claposis was a code word–
Diane used to say
when she had an ... orgasm ...
so you'd know the difference.
It was a joke.

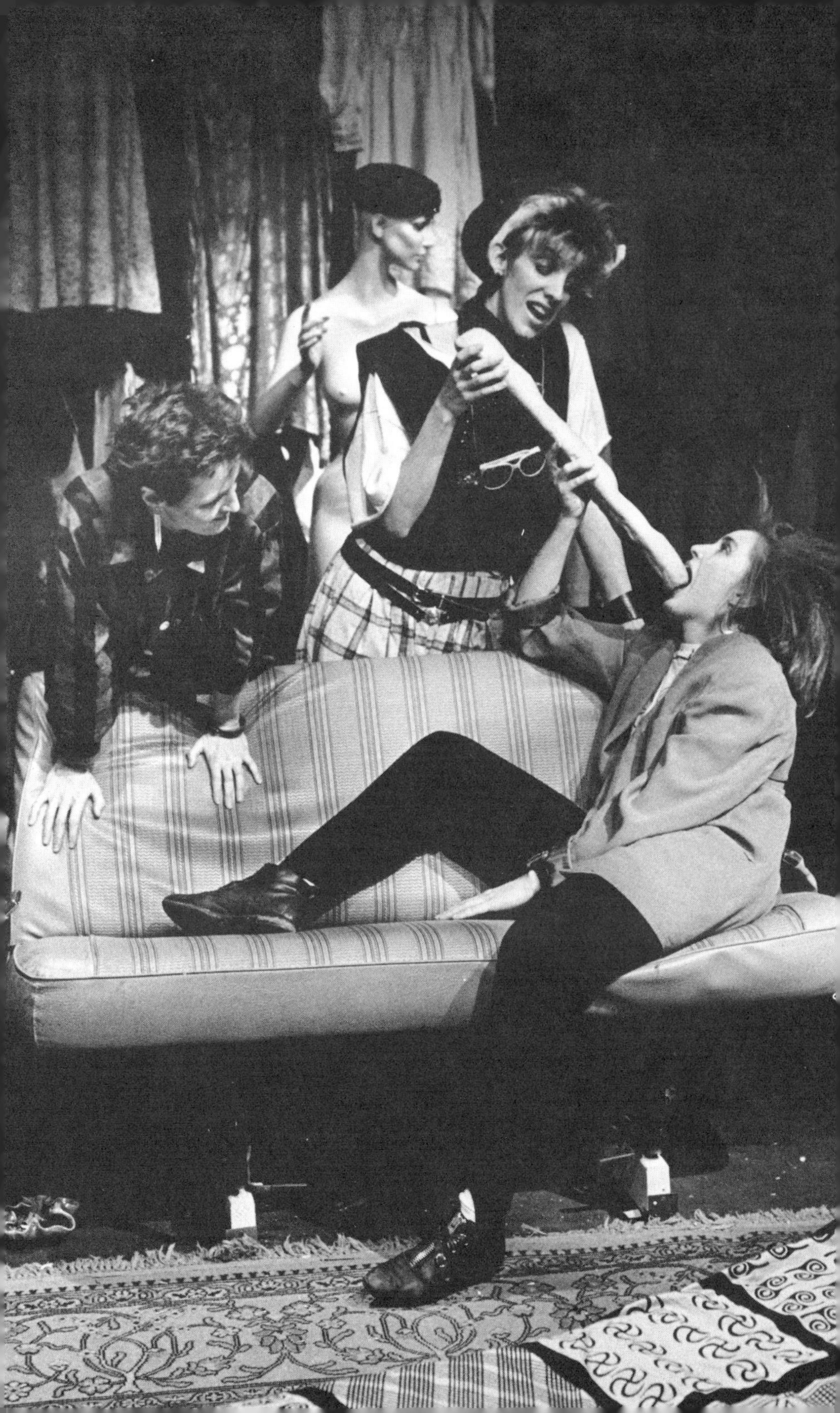

KATE: Well, maybe I should tell people that.

BETH: So what does it really mean?

JUDY: Two waves meeting.
It's a geographical–
or is it oceanographical?–
term for two waves meeting–
for that phenomenon.
Happens in tidal pools or something,
doesn't it, Kate?

KATE: Sounds boring–
most people think
it's a really exotic disease–

BETH: I don't think it's boring–
A bit too close to home maybe–

KATE: Exactly–

BETH: But not boring.

JUDY: I like my definition, though–
just think,
if you open up a chain of stores
you could call them Claposi.
Think of the stories
you could tell people then,
whew!!

KATE: Live sex food, huh?
Mind giving me a hand
in the kitchen for a minute?

Kate and Judy exit.

BETH: This is too much.
I don't know how much longer I can stand it.
Being in the same room with these two.
They might as well be making love
right in front of me.
Oh, god, why am I being so selfish.
They're in love, for godsake.
If Faith were here she'd probably...
pretend it wasn't happening.
Like she pretended what happened

between us didn't really happen.
We only made love once
in the two years we were roommates.
On her birthday.
All we did before then was talk about it.
Talk about it for three hours
and fall asleep in each other's arms,
exhausted.
She before me, usually.
And I was left weighing the pros and cons
of taking advantage of her
right there and then.
Of course I never did.
I didn't want her to hate me.
Or worse, pretend it never happened.
That would just kill me.
Why did I have to get that letter?
Why does she keep sending them
after all these years!
I want her to stop.
Stop torturing me!

Judy enters.

JUDY: Beth?

BETH: What?

JUDY: You okay?

Beth nods.

You're not mad at me too, are you?

BETH: No. Why? Is Kate mad at you?

JUDY: She got over it.

BETH: I'm sorry–

JUDY: It's okay.

BETH: I think we better help with dinner. Kate.

KATE: *(Offstage)* Yes?

BETH: Anything we can do?

KATE: Put some music on.

Beth does. Beth and Judy dance to Wanda Jackson's "Fujiyama Mama" Kate enters, watches in amusement. Beth and Judy kiss. Kate turns away.

BLACKOUT/MUSIC

SCENE NINE
Kate in back room of Claposis. Judy enters.

JUDY: Jeezus!
It's freezing out there!

KATE: You should've just called me.

JUDY: I was in the neighbourhood.
I'm meeting Beth at the Wheat.
She quit her job today.

KATE: Is she all right?

JUDY: I don't know. Probably not.

KATE: Oh–

JUDY: I know I said I'd come over later.

KATE: Don't you think you better
check with her first?

JUDY: Kate–

KATE: Better not keep her waiting–

JUDY: We could see each other later–

KATE: Beth is more important right now–

JUDY: Oh, god.
Listen, she quit her job.
What do you want me to do?

KATE: Beth has been talking about quitting her job for months–

JUDY: Doesn't mean she's not upset, Kate.

KATE: Oh, I know.
Better not keep her waiting.

JUDY: You're not jealous, are you?

KATE: No, no.
I've got a lot of things on my mind–

JUDY: Like what? Kate, what's wrong?

KATE: Nothing.
You've got Beth's problems to deal with.
You don't need to hear about mine–

JUDY: What problems?
Kate.
Tell me.

KATE: Problems with the store–

JUDY: What kinda problems?
Money problems?

KATE: Not really.

JUDY: What then?

KATE: The landlord's selling the building.

Pause

JUDY: Oh.
When did he tell you that?

KATE: He didn't.

JUDY: So how'd you find out?

KATE: The psychic upstairs has heard rumours–

JUDY: You sure she hasn't been staring into her crystal ball too long?

KATE: Judy!

JUDY: Okay, okay.
Did she happen to catch on to who was buying it?

KATE: The condo vultures.
They're buying up the whole block–

JUDY: Every building on this street has heard that rumour–

KATE: I know, but–

JUDY: But what?

KATE: I have this awful premonition
that I'm going to lose Claposis.

JUDY: Just don't think about it right now, okay?
Nothing you can do till you know for sure,
is there?

Pause

Listen, I'll call you later.
Beth's waiting–

KATE: Oh, Beth, right.

JUDY: Kate–

KATE: Mustn't keep Beth waiting–

JUDY: Don't start–

KATE: Beth's quit her job–

JUDY: Come on–

KATE: That's more important.

JUDY: You know that's not true.

KATE: How do I know it's not true?

JUDY: Kate!
She needs me!

KATE: Well, maybe–just once–I need you too!

JUDY: I can't be two fucking places at once, can I?

KATE: Exactly.

JUDY: So whadda ya want me to do, Kate?
Just leave her there in some bar
'cause some batty psychic told you a fucking rumour?
She quit her job, Kate
because she couldn't take the baiting anymore.
You ever heard of gay baiting?
How would you like it if some numbskull breeder
stuck his face in your face every day:
Are you a dyke, honey?
Do you eat smelly pussy?
Boy, I'd really like to see you and your girlfriend
making out sometime!

KATE: I–I–I–didn't know–

JUDY: Well, now you know.

KATE: Why didn't you tell me?

JUDY: Christ, she could hardly tell me.
She made me promise not to tell anyone.
Especially you.

KATE: Me?
We've never even met.

JUDY: Well, she knows how close you and I are now.

KATE: Oh, I see.

JUDY: Oh, Kate, I wish you could meet her.

KATE: I want to. Someday.

JUDY: You two have a lot in common, y'know.
Besides me, I mean.

KATE: How so?

JUDY: You'll find out when you meet.
I could invite her over for dinner.

KATE: Oh, sure–

JUDY: It wouldn't be too awkward?

KATE: No-o-o-o–

JUDY: *(Putting her coat on)* Good.
I'll talk to her about it when I see her–

KATE: Okay.

JUDY: Bye.

KATE: Bye.

> *Judy stomps her foot at the door.*
> *Kate turns back.*

KATE: What?

JUDY: You didn't hug me yet.

BLACKOUT/MUSIC

SCENE TEN

> *Judy in Beth's apartment*
> *sitting up in bed reading,*
> *listening to "Fujiyama Mama."*
> *Beth enters, turns off the music.*

JUDY: Hi.

BETH: Hi.

JUDY: Did'ja have a good time tonight?

BETH: Yeah. Why?

JUDY: You seemed kinda down.

BETH: Yeah.
Must be work.

JUDY: If it's that bad, quit.

BETH: I wish that asshole would quit!

JUDY: Why doesn't somebody fire the motherfucker?

BETH: Because he's Mr. Keith's sister's husband–

JUDY: Who's that?

BETH: Mr. Keith, my boss–

JUDY: He's your boss's sister's–

BETH: His sister's hus–

JUDY: Brother-in-law–

BETH: Right.
So I guess I better quit.

JUDY: Do it.
Before I go down and shoot the bastard.

BETH: What are you reading?

JUDY: It was on the bed–

BETH: Judy! Those are personal–

JUDY: They're good, Beth.
You should do a reading.

BETH: Who would sit through them?

JUDY: I would.

BETH: They're too personal–
self-indulgent shit.

JUDY: What about this one?
The one about the legs–
I bet that one's about you-know-who, huh?

BETH: Who?

JUDY: You know who.

BETH: Who?

JUDY: Me!

BETH: Well, not just you–
other people too–

JUDY: Other lovers?
Is Jeffy in here?

Beth takes notebook

Ahhh! Let me read it!

BETH: Why?

JUDY: Because–because I let you read my stuff.
Let me read it, please?
Please?

Pause

Oh, forget it, I don't wanna read it anyway.

BETH: I can't understand why you're so jealous of Jeff.

JUDY: Jealous?
Of Jeff?
Why should I be?

BETH: Exactly.

JUDY: For one thing:
I'm a better writer than he is.
And for another thing:
I'm not a pervert–

BETH: Judy!

JUDY: Well, it's true!
Not a word of a lie
and you know it.
I can't believe he set you up like that
just to get his rocks off.
I'd never set you up with Kate.

BETH: Why not?
Anyway, it wasn't like that–

JUDY: Oh! It wasn't like that!
Gimme a break!

BETH: I'm not as naive as you think.
I knew exactly what I was doing.

JUDY: You wanted it to happen?

BETH: For a long time
I couldn't bring myself

| | to sleep with another woman
because of what happened with Faith.
Maybe you should be grateful to Jeff
instead of jealous– |
| --- | --- |
| JUDY: | Would you feel like making love
if Jeff was in the room wankin' off? |
| BETH: | That's really stupid, Judy.
Not to mention insulting! |
| JUDY: | Then how come you have to get drunk
whenever we do fuck, huh? |
| BETH: | That's not fair.
You are, too,
usually. |
| JUDY: | I don't want it to be like that anymore. |
| BETH: | Is that why you're still seeing Kate?
Cause she's so...stable? |
| JUDY: | Maybe. |
| BETH: | Good. Good.
I'm glad you found someone,
cause I'm just too fucked up.
I don't know why I'm fucked up,
but I just can't seem to do anything about it right now
and you knew that when we started sleeping together
so I don't feel guilty.
I'm going to sleep! |
| JUDY: | Beth,
I don't want you to feel guilty.
I just wanna ... make love. |

Beth snores
Judy slaps her on the ass

BLACKOUT/MUSIC

SCENE ELEVEN

Kate and Judy moving into the back room.

JUDY: *(Holding up the birdcage)* Ka-a-aty-y-y!!!!

KATE: *(Offstage)* What, honey?

JUDY: Where do you want the birds?

KATE: Oh, I don't know.
Anywhere.

> *Judy finds a place.*
> *Kate sneaks up behind Judy, gooses her.*

JUDY: Hey!
Hey!
What's goin' on?

> *They chase each other around.*

Don't tickle me!
No!
Don't tickle me!!

KATE: Hey.
There's a bottle of wine in one of those boxes
in the kitchen.
We should celebrate.

JUDY: Okay.
Oh no, I better call Beth.
We're supposed to have lunch today.

KATE: Will she mind?

JUDY: I don't think so.
But it was my idea.

KATE: You better go, then.

JUDY: I'll call her, okay.
See what she says.

> *Judy dials.*
> *Phone rings in Beth's apartment.*

BETH: Hello.

JUDY: Hi.

BETH: Oh, hi!

JUDY: Listen, hon.
You really wanna do lunch today?

BETH: It doesn't really–

JUDY: The reason I'm askin' is:
I'm helpin' Kate move into her store–
Claposis–
today.
Could we do it next week?

BETH: I thought–

JUDY: What?
What's wrong?

BETH: I didn't realize you two were–
I mean I thought–
it was only that once.

JUDY: Oh.

Pause

No,
we've been seeing a lot of each other–

BETH: Oh.
Well,
don't let her bite you–

JUDY: What?

BETH: Nothing–
Call me next week.

JUDY: You okay?

BETH: Yeah.
Don't forget to call me.

JUDY: I won't.
Bye.

Judy hangs up.

BETH: She's the one who bites
I'm the one
who tastes like apples.
I'm the one
you said you loved.

Beth hangs up.

What's going to happen to us?

KATE: So what's going to happen to us?

JUDY: Who the fuck knows?

MUSIC/BLACKOUT
♦♦♦

ACKNOWLEDGEMENTS

The author would like to thank the following individuals and organizations for their support, both financial and emotional, before, during and after both productions of *Claposis* in 1985: Robert Scott, Shelley Ledger, Ellen Ray Hennessy, Siobhan McCormick, Larkin Timney, Sky Gilbert, Buddies in Bad Times Theatre, Theatre Passe Muraille, Bersani & Carlevale – The Atrium, Free Times Cafe, Darcy Atkinson, Lorri Millan, Sharon E. H. Norris (graphics), Betsy Carey (publicity photos), Donna Marchand (4-Play production photographer), *Xtra!* and *NOW* magazines, Tannis Atkinson, Bob Welsh, Michael Fitzgerald and Larry Fineberg.

ABOUT THE PLAYWRIGHT

Audrey Butler is currently co-artistic director of Tempermental Journey, a playwright-centred company based in Toronto and Lanark, Nova Scotia, with her partner in theatrical crimes, Bryden MacDonald. She is the author of *Shakedown, Cradle Pin, Claposis, Vinyl Hearts, The Watercooler Incident* (a ten-minute two-hander), *Black Friday?* and *Medusa Rising*. Audrey has been playwright-in-residence at Kam Theatre Lab, Thunder Bay (1985) and Theatre Passe Muraille, Toronto (1989/90 season). She is the co-creator of *Late Nite Lesbians: The Talk-Show*, complete with Stupid Lesbian Tricks and the Lesbian Sex questionnaire. She has written articles, reviews, etc. for *Rites* and *Canplay*. Her first published piece was a poem about her period for *The Other Woman* when she was seventeen. Audrey hopes to start writing in prose soon with more radical perversions called *Leztrash*. Audrey is looking forward to taking her pleasure into her own hands way into the/her 90s.